OPTICAL ILLUSIONS

FOR QUILTERS

Karen Combs

Located in Paducah, Kentucky, the American Quilter's Society (AQS), is dedicated to promoting the accomplishments of today's quilters. Through its publications and events, AQS strives to honor today's quiltmakers and their work — and inspire future creativity and innovation in quiltmaking.

EDITOR: MARY JO KURTEN
TECHNICAL EDITOR: HELEN SQUIRE
BOOK DESIGN/ILLUSTRATIONS: WHITNEY HOPKINS
COVER DESIGN: TERRY WILLIAMS
PHOTOGRAPHY: CHARLES R. LYNCH

Library of Congress Cataloging-in-Publication Data

Combs, Karen.
    Optical illusions for quilters / Karen Combs.
      p.   cm.
    Includes bibliographical references.
    ISBN 0-89145-892/1
    1. Patchwork--Patterns. 2. Quilting--Patterns. 3. Optical
illusions in art. I. Title.
    TT835.C649   1997
    746.46'041--dc21   97-30330
                                                CIP

Additional copies of this book may be ordered from: American Quilter's Society, PO Box 3290, Paducah, KY 42002-3290 @ $22.95 Add $2.00 for postage & handling.

Printed in the U.S.A. by Image Graphics, Paducah, KY

DEDICATION

This book is dedicated
to my grandmother,
Dora Andrews Bensinger
(1911-1995).

My Grandma gave me my first scrap bag and always supported me in whatever I did. When I began to write, she said, "Well, I can't decide whether you are going to be a quilter or a writer. You do both so well." Grandma, now I am both!

ACKNOWLEDGMENTS

To my husband, Rick: Thank you for your help and patience while I worked on this tremendous and wonderful project.

To my children, Angela and Josh: Thank you for your help in picking up the slack around the house, and thank you for your understanding when I said, "Just a minute, I'm in the middle of a thought and need to write it down."

I love you all!

No book is ever created without the help and support of many people. I wish to thank the Maury Quilters' Guild of Columbia, Tennessee, for their support and help in producing this book.

This book would not be complete without the work of the many quilt artists who shared their quilts with me. My special thanks to each of them. They are truly Masters of Illusion!

Charlotte Warr Andersen, Deanna Smith Apfel, Mary Beth Bellah, Nancy S. Brown, Elizabeth A. Bush, Pat Coulter, Sandra Townsend Donabed, Adabelle Dremann, Ellen Anne Eddy, Cynthia England, Wendy D. Etzel, Caryl Bryer Fallert, Bobbie Fuhrmann, Fiona Gavens, Beth Gillaspy, Carol Goddu, Alison Goss, Marjorie B. Hansen, Irma Gail Hatcher, Wendy Hill, Lois K. Ide, Catherine McConnell, Katherine L. McKean, Barbara Barrick McKie, Dianne Miller, Sally Nadelman, Glenys R. Nappo, Jean Neblett, Jan Myers-Newbury, Kathleen O'Connor, Virginia Ferrill Piland, Donna Radner, Amanda Richardson, Emily Richardson, Lucretia Romey, Heather Rose, Georgia Schmidt, Becky Steinmetz, Eileen Sullivan, Elsie Vredenburg, Edith Zimmer.

Thank you to the terrific staff at AQS who made this book a reality. I wish to especially thank Mary Jo Kurten, Helen Squire, and Rhonda Steele. It was a pleasure working with you!

A special thank you to Barbara Brackman. Without her wonderful book, *Encyclopedia of Pieced Quilt Patterns*, I could not have researched traditional quilt blocks for this book.

PREFACE

Optical illusions are simply pictures that play tricks on your eyes. Depending on the light, the viewing angle, or the way the picture is drawn, you will see things that are not as they appear. Scientists have studied optical illusions for centuries, but still don't agree about how or why they work.

Each section of the book explores a different type of optical illusion, shows how to achieve it, and presents masterpiece quilts and traditional quilt blocks using that illusion. Patterns are included for traditional quilt blocks, and a contemporary quilt.

Read this book from cover to cover or skip right to an illusion that interests you; each section stands on its own. However, the section Illusions of Color contains information helpful in producing all illusions.

This book is meant for the intermediate quilter and does not include basic quilting information. There are many wonderful books on basic quiltmaking to help you get started and move into more detailed work with illusions.

The reference numbers after some of the quilt blocks are identification numbers from *Encyclopedia of Pieced Quilt Patterns* by Barbara Brackman. This number will help you find particular blocks in that reference book. If possible, use *Block Base*, an electric version of Barbara's encyclopedia, in conjuction with this book. You can see each quilt pattern in a grayscale coloring, an antique block coloring, and a contemporary coloring. You can also print out quilt blocks in any size you wish. If you use *Block Base* along with *The Electric Quilt 3.0* software program, you can make unique quilts by playing with blocks to create different illusions.

Let's get started.

INTRODUCTION

Optical illusions have always fascinated me; my first quilts were Kaleidoscope, Tumbling Blocks, and Storm at Sea. However, because I was a self-taught quilter having no formal art background, I was lost about how to create them.

It did not matter. Quilts of illusion called to me, challenging and taunting me until I undertook a study of how to create them. This book is the result of that study, my quest for creating illusions.

Optical Illusions for Quilters is meant for anyone interested in creating illusions; the quilt artist, the artist working with pen and paper or paint, the fiber artist, the art student, all will benefit from this information.

CONTENTS

DEVICES TO SHOW DEPTH

"He who has imagination without learning has wings and no feet."
                                          Joseph Joubert

In two dimensional art forms such as drawings, painting, or wall quilts, the artist often wants to express a feeling of space or depth. The space is an illusion, for the images depicted on paper, canvas or in fabric are indeed flat.

How can we achieve the look of depth on this flat surface? There are many devices that can be used to accomplish the illusion of depth and space. Let's explore each and see how they can be applied to our quiltmaking.

DEPTH CUE: SIZE

The easiest way to create an illusion of space or distance is through the use of size. Very early in life, we observe the visual phenomenon that objects, as they get farther away, appear to become smaller. The shapes are identical; only their sizes are different (Illustration 1-1).

When I was a child, we traveled from Michigan to California to visit relatives. I was enchanted by this phenomenon as I observed the huge power lines that ran across the plains in the Midwest. My brother and I called them "monsters," and we could see them for miles as they marched across the flat terrain, getting smaller and smaller as they disappeared at the horizon.

We can use this device effectively and easily in our quilting. First, let's take a look at some quilts that use size to give the illusion of depth.

The quilt SENTINELS by Charlotte Warr Andersen uses this illusion exceptionally well (Plate I-1). As one depth cue, Charlotte uses different sizes of cactus to give us a sense of depth in her quilt. When size changes are used as in this quilt, the sense of space becomes extremely clear.

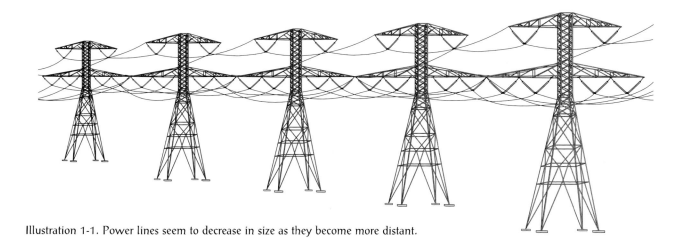

Illustration 1-1. Power lines seem to decrease in size as they become more distant.

DEVICES TO SHOW DEPTH

Plate I-1. SENTINELS, 1990, 94" x 46", Charlotte Warr Andersen, Salt Lake City, Utah. Charlotte hand appliquéd the cactus to the sky background and hand quilted this large wall quilt. The scene is so realistic, that we almost feel we can step right into it. Photo by Ken Wagner.

Plate I-2. PATHWAYS, 1993, 49" x 49", Alison Goss, Cumming, Iowa. Alison used machine paper piecing, hand appliqué, and machine quilting to construct this wonderful quilt with great depth. Photo by Alison Goss.

Size differences to give a feeling of depth are not confined to realistic quilts or painting. The quilt PATHWAYS, made by Alison Goss, uses size beautifully as a depth cue (Plate I-2). The paths create a deep space as they decrease in size and wind their way into the distance. Alison's inspiration arose from two months spent hiking in the San Juan Mountains of southern Colorado. She spent every evening sketching ideas that had come while walking.

You can effectively use size as a depth cue even with abstract shapes, where the forms have no literal meaning or representational quality. When you use abstract shapes, it is best to use the same shape repeated in various sizes.

When different shapes are used in various sizes, you can see the feeling of depth is diminished or nonexistent. All you observe are the various shapes arranged on a flat surface. The feeling of depth is just not there. For the depth cue of size to work, you must use the same shape repeated in different sizes.

Squares in various sizes can also create a sense of space. In Illustration 1-2 you see the smaller squares begin to recede and a spatial pattern appear. This is a simple yet effective way to create depth in quilts. Different size quilt blocks would create this same effect.

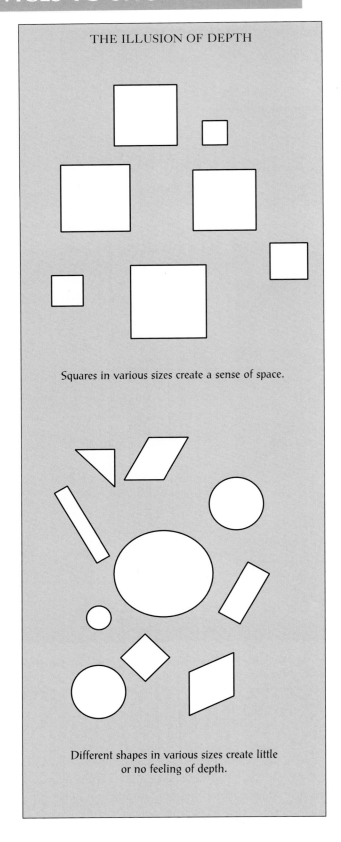

THE ILLUSION OF DEPTH

Squares in various sizes create a sense of space.

Different shapes in various sizes create little or no feeling of depth.

Illustration 1-2. Ohio Star quilt blocks in various sizes create a sense of depth or space.

Plate I-3. YELLOW IRIS LAWSON'S POND, 1989, 59" x 47", Amanda Richardson, Cornwall, United Kingdom. Amanda's exquisite work displays the illusion of great spatial depth. Photo by Amanda Richardson.

Using different sizes to give a feeling of space or depth is very common to many periods and styles of art. Some artists have taken this basic idea and exaggerated it by increasing the size differences.

In the quilt YELLOW IRIS LAWSON'S POND by Amanda Richardson (Plate I-3), the iris flowers in the foreground are in a very large scale and seem quite close. By contrast, the small trees, tiny irises, and ripples in the water seem far off in the distance.

These are two advantages to this practice. First, seeing some irises drawn many times larger than the tiny background irises automatically forces us to image the distance involved. Second, the contrast of large and small items can create a dynamic visual pattern.

Amanda works in a method that can be termed fiber collage. She hand dyes much of her fabric and then applies glue to the back of her fabric. The fabric is then cut into intricate pieces before they are put together to form the final image.

TRADITIONAL QUILT BLOCKS THAT ILLUSTRATE DEPTH BY THE USE OF SIZE

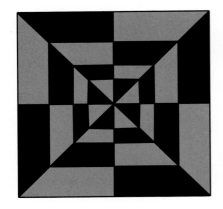

Market Square 1289

Old Maid's Puzzle 1317

Cups and Saucers 1663**

Gentleman's Fancy 2938

Double Square 2029

Mosaic #16 2123

** indicates blocks in pattern section

There are many traditional quilt blocks that use the device of size to create the illusion of depth.

These quilt blocks achieve depth because of the quilt blocks themselves and the effect may be lost if the blocks are set side by side.

These quilt blocks are good patterns to play with. Try placing them in different settings and see if you can still maintain the illusion of depth.

TRADITIONAL QUILT BLOCKS THAT ILLUSTRATE DEPTH WHEN SET SIDE BY SIDE

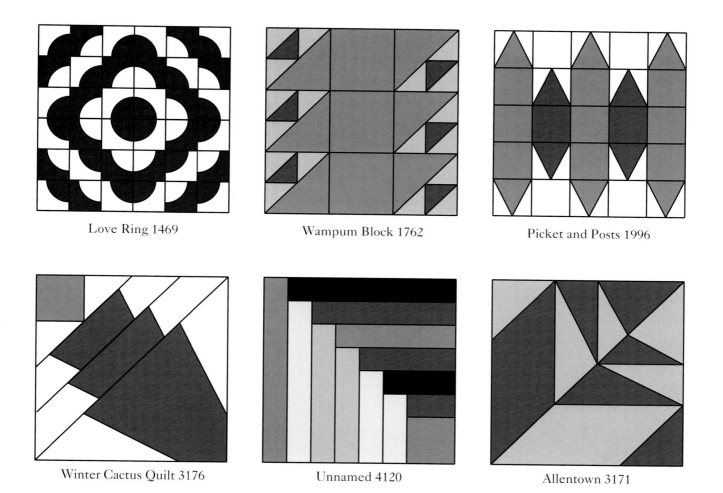

Love Ring 1469

Wampum Block 1762

Picket and Posts 1996

Winter Cactus Quilt 3176

Unnamed 4120

Allentown 3171

These quilt blocks show the illusion of depth by the use of size. They achieve this illusion when set together.

THE ILLUSION OF DEPTH

No depth is shown in these three separate shapes.

When the three shapes ore overlapped, the illusion of depth appears.

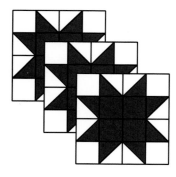

Ohio Star quilt blocks have the illusion of depth when they are overlapped.

DEPTH CUE: OVERLAP

Perhaps the most uncomplicated device to show depth is overlap, the illusion of one shape seeming to interrupt or block our view of another.

Three separate shapes are shown here and the images are flat; no depth is presented. However, as soon as they are overlapped, the illusion of depth appears.

When we use overlapping to suggest depth, the object that is overlapped will always appear more distant, so we can easily obtain depth in our picture. We can use this principle with traditional quilt blocks such as the Ohio Star. In the quilt below, a traditional quilt block is overlapped and depth is achieved.

Early Renaissance paintings used this depth cue

This quilt illustrates the illusion of depth by overlapping traditional star blocks.

Plate I-4. SOUTHERN EXPOSURE, 1994, 49" x 60", Nancy S. Brown, Oakland, California. Nancy created this quilt to depict an imaginary scene of Adelie and Emperor penguins somewhere in Antarctica. Photo by AQS.

exclusively. Overlapping forms were the only guides to read any depth into a painting. The more distant figures were not smaller than those in front, as in a perspective drawing, they were merely overlapped.

In Nancy S. Brown's quilt SOUTHERN EXPOSURE, the grouping of penguins ready to dive is shown with no real size difference between them (Plate I-4). However, we do understand their respective positions because of the overlapping that hides portions of the figures in front and in back. Notice that when overlapping is combined with size differences, as with the penguins in the upper left of the picture, the spatial sensation is greatly increased.

Nancy's quilt also shows the illusion of motion in the border. Notice the anticipated motions of the penquins tobogganing.

Plate I-5. PARIS '76, 1991, 72" x 54", Dianne Miller, North Attleboro, Massachusetts. A beautiful example of overlap to portray depth. While in Paris, Dianne came upon an Yves St. Laurent photo shoot and was inspired to make this quilt. Collection of International Quilt Festival. Photo by Paul A. Miller.

Overlapping untangles what might otherwise be visually vague. By allowing the eye a way to step into the space, overlapping keeps this shallow, packed space from becoming flat.

In THE GILGAMESH TAPESTRY by Virginia Ferrill Pilard, notice the overlap within the multiple figures is purposely avoided and the image is flattened (Plate VI-1, page 98). Very few depth cues for a three-dimensional reading are given. We tend to look up and down the surface, but have difficulty stepping into the space. The shapes look like they are pressed flat.

By contrast, in the quilt PARIS '76 by Dianne Miller (Plate I-5), we see depth and notice a feeling of depth around each form. The bottom woman overlaps both the second and third figures, clearly putting her in front of the voluminous skirt of the second woman. The middle figure's shoulder overlaps the third figure, locating her in the middle distance, and so on. The eye can pick its way through the space by reading each overlapping figure. Each form has a secure place in this space.

Dianne hand appliquéd and hand quilted this beautiful quilt. It is embellished with embroidery and Pigma pen.

Plate I-6. ODE TO NICOLE, 1995, 36" x 36", Karen Combs, Columbia, Tennessee. Intertwining sashing overlaps an enlarged quilt block and creates the illusions of depth in this interesting quilt. Photo by Charles R. Lynch, American Quilter's Society.

Not only do we see the use of overlapping in realistic scenes or pictorial quilts, we also see this tool used in traditional geometric quilts.

My quilt ODE TO NICOLE uses the same principle of overlapping to show depth (Plate I-6). An interwoven grid overlaps the enlarged quilt block, Depression, and a sense of depth is established. The depth is further enhanced by overlapping floral shapes that are placed at the bottom edge of the quilt.

TRADITIONAL QUILT BLOCKS THAT GIVE THE ILLUSION OF DEPTH BY USING OVERLAP I

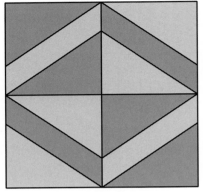

Left and Right 1188

Night and Day 1218

The Scottish Cross 1220

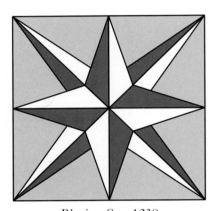

Blazing Star 1238

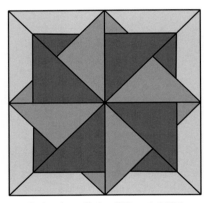

Spinning Color Wheel 1295

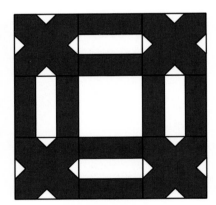

Cross Roads 1753

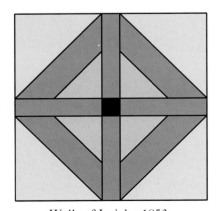

Walls of Jericho 1853

Paths to Piece 3264

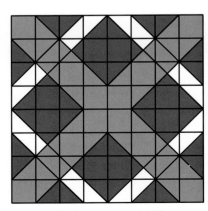

Gothic pattern 1167

TRADITIONAL QUILT BLOCKS THAT GIVE THE ILLUSION OF DEPTH BY USING OVERLAP II

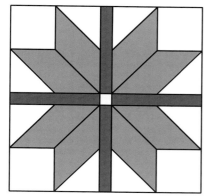

The E-Z Quilt 1895

Irish Plaid 2558

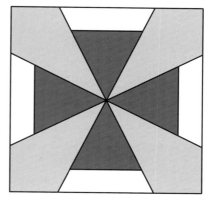

The Pinwheel 2718

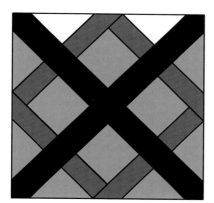

The Coverlet 3262

Diamond Knot 4202

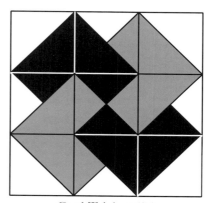

Card Tricks 1674

DEPTH
CUE:
GRADIENTS

Gradients are effective tools for creating pictorial space. A gradient is any gradual, orderly, step-by-step change in some visual feature. You may already be familiar with this technique. We see this method used in the traditional quilt pattern Flying Geese. This design is the back of Caryl Bryer Fallert's quilt, MIGRATIONS #2 (Plate I-7, page 21). You see the triangles gradually deceasing in size as they move toward the center.

For this tool to be effective, the change in a gradient must happen in a fairly even series of steps. There must be enough steps so the eye does not have to jump, and the intervals must be reasonably smooth. The sense of depth is weakened when there are not enough steps.

If the steps are not even, as you see in Illustration 1-3, you tend to see a small form next to a large one, instead of a distant and a near form.

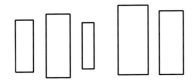

Illustration 1-3. The steps in this gradient are not even, so you see a small form next to a large one rather than depth.

Generally, as more and clearer gradients are added, the illusion of depth and volume is strengthened. In Illustration 1-4, I've also added shading to increase the illusion of depth.

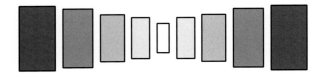

Illustration 1-4. The illusion of depth is strengthened when an even progression is used. The illusion is increased by the added shading.

In the figures below, the use of gradients is clearly evident. The gradually decreasing triangles in Illustration 1-5 show depth as they progress toward the center of the design. We see even greater depth in Illustration 1-6 with the use of gradually decreasing rectangles. We also see an illusion of motion with the use of these repeat figures.

Illustration 1-5. Gradually decreasing triangles show depth as they progress toward the center of the design.

Illustration 1-6. Greater depth is displayed with the use of gradually decreasing rectangles in this design.

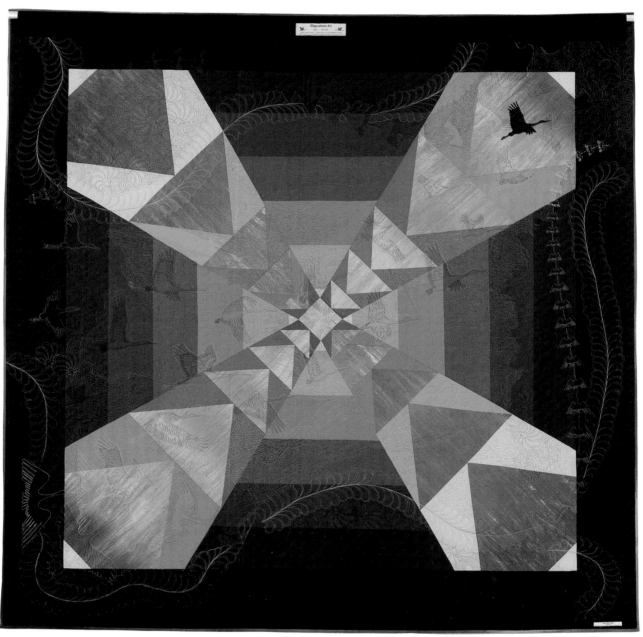

Plate I-7. MIGRATIONS #2, 1993, 89" x 88", Caryl Bryer Fallert, Oswego, Illinois. The back of MIGRATIONS #2 is an original variation of Flying Geese in the form of one 72" radially symmetrical block. The block gives a beautiful illusion of depth using gradients. Photo by Richard Walker, from the collection of the Museum of the American Quilter's Society (MAQS).

TRADITIONAL QUILT BLOCKS THAT SHOW DEPTH BY THE USE OF GRADIENTS

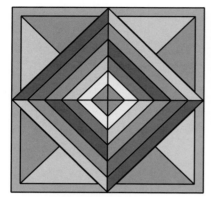

Peter's Quilt 1229

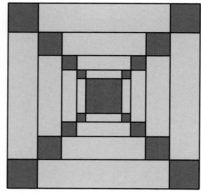

Squares and Oblongs 2025**

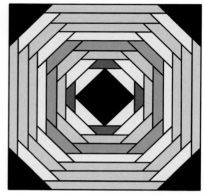

Pineapple 2635

Modern Flame 3177

Chevrons 3178

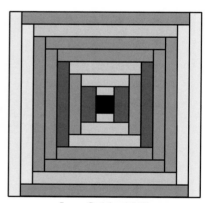

Log Cabin 3240

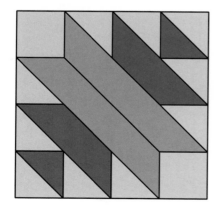

Mrs. Taft's Choice 3271

** indicates blocks in pattern section

"Art is the appearance of effortlessness and the perfectly right choice. What is hidden are the sloppy paint cans, the crumpled pages on the floor, the cancelled ideas and impulses."
Author unknown

DEPTH CUE: VERTICAL LOCATION

Vertical location is a device you see all the time without noticing it. It is based on a visual fact. Let's examine the illusion of depth using vertical location as we look at Illustration 1-7.

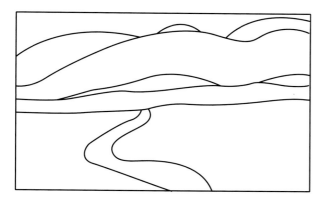

Illustration 1-7. Depth is shown in this drawing by use of vertical location.

Imagine you are actually standing at this scene. Notice the closest thing to your feet is the road, located at the bottom of the picture. As you gradually raise your eyes, the foothills move farther away. They are located at eye level, or what is called the horizon. The horizon reference is an integral part of vertical location. Here, it is located in the middle of the picture. As you look farther away, the mountains against the sky are located in the upper part of the scene.

Artists, for many years, have manipulated space or depth using this technique. They use the bottom of the picture field as near and the top as farther away.

You do the same thing whenever you look at a photograph, realistic painting, or quilt. You expect the foreground to be at the lower part of the visual field and the forms in the distance to occur higher up.

VERTICAL LOCATION AS A DEPTH CUE IN QUILT BLOCKS

There are very few quilt blocks that use vertical location to suggest depth. You will find this tool more widely used in pictorial quilts. However, I did find one quilt block that has the suggestion of depth with the use of vertical location.

I recommend Barbara Brackman's *Encyclopedia of Pieced Quilt Patterns*, *BlockBase*, an electronic version of *Encyclopedia of Pieced Quilt Patterns*, and *The Electric Quilt* computer software for patterns. They are available at local bookstores and quilt shops.

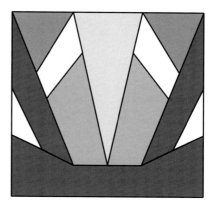

Northern Lights 4139

Plate I-8. SPLIT ROCK SUNSET, 1996, 53" x 59", Elsie Vredenburg, Tustin, Michigan. Elsie captures the beautiful essence of Split Rock though she has never been there herself. Using the depth cues, vertical location and overlap, the quilt has a sense of space and depth. Photo by Charles R. Lynch, American Quilter's Society.

We see this device, vertical location, used in the quilt by Elsie Vredenburg, SPLIT ROCK SUNSET (Plate I-8). Notice the water at the bottom of the quilt, the horizon is in the middle and the sky is located at the top of the quilt — a classic use of vertical location to illustrate depth. However, depth is also illustrated by the use of overlap. We see Split Rock overlapping both the water and the sky, and we sense depth. This quilt also has an excellent example of a horizon line, the point where sky and land or sea meet. Horizon line is discussed in detail in Chapter 3.

Plate I-9. THREE SISTERS, 1994, Janine Holzman. Janine uses vertical location to illustrate great depth in her quilt. It is an excellent example of this device and is convincingly real in its illusion of depth. Photo by Janine Holzman.

In THREE SISTERS by Janine Holzman, nearly all space cues are eliminated except for vertical location (Plate I-9). This is a classic example of vertical location; creating a sense of infinite distance at the bottom of the quilt is the water, seemingly at our feet. Midpoint in the quilt is a snow-capped mountain, and at the top of the quilt, the moon and stars appear far away in the sky. The result is a space that is both convincingly real, and satisfying in its harmony and visual richness.

Our experience teaches us that shapes are usually heavier and more numerous nearer the ground and get progressively fewer and lighter as the vision moves up. An intuitive sense of gravity is also involved in this observation.

When we see things rise, a gymnast on the pommel horse or a ball thrown into the air, what we "see" is energy and power being released and gravity overcome.

Illustration courtesy of CorelDRAW™.

Watching something sink to the ground, such as a hot air balloon, is seeing a relaxation or surrender to the downward pull.

Illustration courtesy of CorelDRAW™.

Because of these well-learned visual observations, the top of a visual field feels a little different from the bottom, and shapes look a little different when placed high or low.

DEPTH CUE: TOP AND BOTTOM

The concept of top and bottom follows vertical location. Still looking at the lower and upper parts of our picture field, there are other things to notice.

The upper and lower parts of any visual field are different. To illustrate this point, divide a square horizontally into two exactly equal rectangles and notice how the upper one seems slightly larger or heavier (Illustration 1-8).

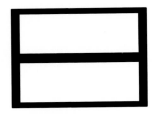

Illustration 1-8. This square is equally divided into two sections, but the upper one seems slightly larger.

Artists can place shapes to achieve a neutral balance, or a visual evenness, between top and bottom. For example, imagine cutting a rectangular opening in a mat with borders all the same width. The opening will seem to be placed too low. If the bottom margin is made slightly wider than the one above, the placement of the drawing will feel more comfortable (Illustration 1-9).

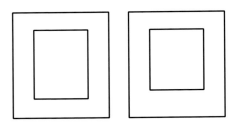

Illustration 1-9. The mat on the left seems off balance. A neutral balance can be achieved by placing the opening slightly higher as illustrated by the mat on the right.

Optical Illusions for Quilters

Plate I-10. DO NOT GO GENTLE, 1993, 53" x 60", Charlotte Warr Andersen, Salt Lake City, Utah. In this serene quilt, a wider bottom border creates a visual evenness in what otherwise could be a top heavy design. Photo by Richard Walker, from the collection of the Museum of the American Quilter's Society.

Charlotte Warr Andersen uses this device effectively in her work DO NOT GO GENTLE (Plate I-10). By using a wider border at the bottom than the top, she creates a visual evenness. She also uses vertical location to suggest depth. Charlotte based this quilt on a photograph her brother Steven took of their father 30 years ago. The man in the quilt is dressed as her father liked to dress.

DEVICES TO SHOW DEPTH

In the twentieth century, we have gained the ability to fly, and the traditional ground-horizon-sky visual reference, or vertical location, has been notably altered. We are accustomed to aerial photographs, or "birds-eye" views, in which the traditional horizon has disappeared. Now the point farthest away from us can be at the bottom of the picture or the ground. Vertical location is still an effective spatial device but may not be as quickly perceived as in the past (Plates I-11 and I-12).

Plates I-11. A New York skyline as seen from the top of the RCA building. Photo by Karen Combs.

Plate I-12. A Toronto view is hauntingly similar to the quilt, CITYSCAPE. Did we happen to stay at the same hotel? Photo by Karen Combs.

Optical Illusions for Quilters

Plate I-13. CITYSCAPE, 1985, 50" x 64", Lucretia Romey, East Orleans, Massachusetts. The view from a seventh floor of a Toronto hotel room inspired this quilt. Photo by AQS.

In the quilt CITYSCAPE by Lucretia Romey, you see this altered vertical location concept used to a great advantage. Lucretia works directly on the backing and fiberfill with strips of fabric. Freehand, she draws the outlines on the fiberfill with a soft lead pencil. She then proceeds to sew and flip. Lucretia is also a painter and prefers this direct approach.

Plate I-14. COUNTRY SCHOOL, 1988, 73" x 92", Adabelle Dremann (1910 – 1992), Princeton, Illinois. A charming example of vertical location using an aerial view. This quilt was partially inspired by the historic "Colton School", a one-room rural schoolhouse in Illinois, and the Grant Wood painting, "Arbor Day." Photo from the collection of the Museum of the American Quilter's Society.

We also see this technique used in the "bird's eye" view in COUNTRY SCHOOL (Plate I-14) by Adabelle Dremann. The original design for this quilt was drawn on 9" x 12" paper. Sections were then enlarged to full size and used as patterns.

USING DEPTH

Ideas must work through the brains and arms of men, or they are not better than dreams.

Ralph Waldo Emerson

PICTORIAL BOX

It's possible to imagine and visualize many kinds of depth in a flat surface. There are always choices and options for one who wants to design with space.

One way of organizing space in Western art has been envisioning the page or the area of your quilt as a pictorial box.

COME INTO THE LIGHT, by Cynthia England, a graphic artist turned quilter, is an excellent example (Plate II-1). The quilt's surface or picture plane, is like a window through which open space is visible. By stressing the beginning of the space, the quilter heightens the effect of entering. She shows the newel post and then carefully constructs a floor pattern that leads the eye inward. You finally arrive at the door that forms the back or outer limits of the space. The decorative archway helps create a space within a space.

Plate II-1. COME INTO THE LIGHT, 1992, 43" x 64", Cynthia England, Houston, Texas. This delightful quilt was inspired by a photograph and constructed using a new freezer paper technique developed for machine piecing by the designer. Photo by Cynthia England.

Plate II-2. IN THE BEGINNING – COLLECTIBLES #1, 1995, 50" x 58", Wendy D. Etzel, Williamsport, Pennsylvania. This quilt is the cover of Wendy's book, <u>The Collectibles Quilt</u>, RCW Publishing. Photo by Terry Wild Studio.

The concept of seeing the surface or picture plane as the entry point into a deeper space is one of the most familiar in the history of Western art. However, despite its limitations, or perhaps because of them, this approach has been a useful one; it keeps things clear. The front, top, bottom, back, and sides are easy to see. It creates a manageable, measurable space that can be as deep or as shallow as required.

The sense of a box space is not only found in illusionist art or perspective drawing. This kind of space is also seen in the work COLLECTIBLES #1 by Wendy Etzel (Plate II-2). This quilt relies on the containing quality of the box, here a bookcase. Shapes overlap the interior of the bookcase and the smaller items are contained on the shelves. They provide the intimate feeling of a collectible cupboard.

Wendy machine pieced, appliquéd, and quilted this charming quilt.

OPEN FORM
CLOSED FORM

Another aspect of pictorial space that concerns the artist or designer is the idea of enclosure; the technique is called open form or closed form. The artist has the choice of giving us a complete scene to view or a partial glimpse of a scene that continues beyond the format.

CLOSED FORM

Enclosed space, the sense of containment, always has a special fascination for the viewer. Artists have found many ways to use enclosed space expressively.

Enclosed space, or closed form, can be more than a framed box shape or a quilt with a border. It draws the eye inward.

CLOSED FORM VS. OPEN FORM

A border is a frame around the perimeter of a quilt that visually turns the eye inward. This frame creates the effect of closed form, no matter what the original design of the art work. Some artists have gone even farther and included painted frames, even lettered titles, as elements within the composition.

Closed form generally gives a rather formal, structured appearance, whereas open form creates a casual, momentary feeling, with elements moving on and off the format in an informal manner.

RECESSION

In discussing pictorial space, one more concept must be discussed — the process of recession into depth.

There are two basic devices. Plane recession shows distance by receding on a series of levels that are parallel to the picture plane. Recession is, therefore, slow and orderly; most of the movement is side to side or up and down.

Diagonal recession occurs when the planes are not flat but recede diagonally, rapidly opening the pictorial space. The movement is now back and forth or in and out. We are not discussing the degree of depth, how deep or shallow the picture is, but just how the recession is achieved.

DIAGONAL RECESSION

When planes are arranged to move in the picture space at an angle to the front plane itself, the image looks quite different. It seems to have more visual motion and feels less enclosed. This means of going through space, sometimes called diagonal recession, can give drama and movement to the most ordinary subject matter.

Plate II-3. WORLD PEACE, 1988, 65" x 65", Lois K. Ide, Bucyrus, Ohio. Lois effectively framed the world with a Trip Around the World setting to create a wonderful example of closed form. Photo by Lois K. Ide.

WORLD PEACE by Lois K. Ide puts the focal point in the center of the composition, and our eyes are not led outside the quilt (Plate II-3).

Lois machine pieced and hand appliquéd this wonderful quilt. It is quilted by hand.

The earth is effectively "framed" by the trip-around-the-world setting and the use of the lighter value fabric around the earth, heightens the effect. Wherever we look, our attention is drawn directly back to the earth, thus "closed form."

Plate II-4. LOOKING FOR THE INNER LIGHT, 96" x 84", Alison Goss, Cumming, Iowa. Alison was inspired to make this wonderful quilt from a series of drawing exercises she did while working through Betty Edward's book, <u>Drawing on the Artist Within</u>. Photo by Richard Walker.

LOOKING FOR THE INNER LIGHT (Plate II-4), by Alison Goss uses light to dark gradients and a composition that rotates like a snail shell around its center to move the eye from larger foreground units to smaller background ones. Here, the sense of enclosure is created by the composition turning in on itself and the contrast of light and dark.

Plate II-5. VAN DER GRINTEN VISION, 1988, 61" x 41", Becky Steinmetz, St. Louis, Missouri. An innovative interpretation of attic windows provides an excellent example of open form. Photo by Becky Steinmetz.

OPEN FORM By contrast, Becky Steinmetz's quilt, VAN DER GRINTEN VISION (Plate II-5) is clearly "open form." In this work, we see only a partial globe grid which leads the eye off the quilt. In fact, this design almost forces us to think more of the parts we cannot see than of those shown.

Becky was inspired to make this quilt by memories of the large world maps that adorned her childhood school classroom walls. The Van der Grinten projection (curved latitudes and longitudes of a National Geographic Society map) was her basis. Her intent in this quilt was to create a view of the world from a different perspective.

To use open form, visual elements must be organized to create a sense of unenclosed space; space that seems to continue beyond the boundaries of the page or edges of the quilt.

Plate II-6. ACE OF CUPS, 1993, 96" x 98", Kathleen O'Connor, Putney, Vermont. This quilt with attitude has elements that extend beyond a rectangular format and destroy any framed feeling. Sierra Photo – Michael Dixon.

In quilting, we can enhance open form by using quilting lines that lead off the quilt.

The ultimate extension of the open form concept is illustrated in ACE OF CUPS by Kathleen O'Connor (Plate II-6). The quilt has elements that extend beyond a rectangular format and effectively destroy any framed or contained feeling.

Kathleen says she is interested in the tension created by the outer shape of a piece and the sense of depth created within the space. Depth might not be the right word in ACE's case; it seems to expand outward into space more than it recedes into space.

USING DEPTH

TRADITIONAL QUILT BLOCKS THAT CREATE A SENSE OF DEPTH BY THE USE OF CLOSED FORM*

Tennessee Mine Shaft 4124

Northern Lights 4175

*Draws the eye to the center of the block.

TRADITIONAL QUILT BLOCKS THAT CREATE A SENSE OF DEPTH BY THE USE OF OPEN FORM**

Tangled Trails 1554

Blazing Star 2669

Unnamed 1553

**Leads the eye off the "page" or past the edges of the block.

Plate II-7. SHARING THE GOSSIP, 1994, Heather Rose, South Australia. Heather created a quilt that is an excellent example of depth by use of plane recession by use of hand appliqué, machine piecing, and quilting.

PLANE OR FRONTAL RECESSION

In SHARING THE GOSSIP (Plate II-7) by Heather Rose, the figure of the woman is somewhat flat and creates a horizontal plane in front of the flat wall and windows of the restaurant. In the distance a car makes another parallel plane. The plane recession is clear.

Sometimes pictorial space is created by a series of overlapping layers that are parallel to the pictorial plane, like cutout layers of scenery set parallel to the front of a stage. This way of moving into and through a space is called frontal recession. It reminds the viewer of the flat surface even while leading the eye past it into the picture. Each layer of space marks a step into depth and echoes the two-dimensional surface.

TRADITIONAL QUILT BLOCKS THAT SHOW PLANE OR FRONTAL RECESSION

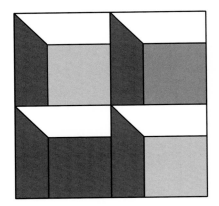

Attic Windows 1366

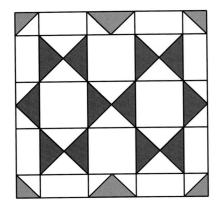

Washington Star 1958

Star X 2835

TRADITIONAL QUILT BLOCKS THAT HAVE A STRONG DIAGONAL RECESSION

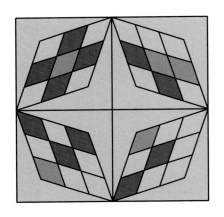

Four Star Block 1245

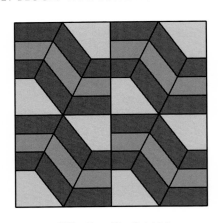

Winding Trail 1424

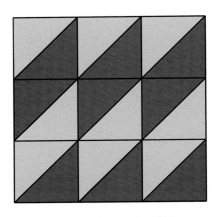

Slanted Diamonds 1692c

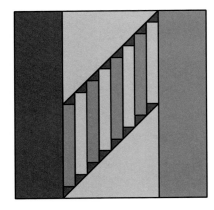

Golden Stairs 3245

Reach high, for stars lie hidden in your soul. Dream deep, for every dream precedes the goal.

Pamela Vaull Starr

Plate II-8. AFTER THE STORM, 1993, 69" x 79", Eileen Sullivan, Alpharetta, Georgia. Eileen foundation pieced, hand appliquéd, and hand quilted this quilt. This beautiful seascape quilt is a wonderful example of diagonal recession and perspective. Photo by Richard Walker.

Plate II-9. Back of AFTER THE STORM.

In AFTER THE STORM (Plate II-8) by Eileen Bahring Sullivan, the emphasis is on diagonals. The beach and the ocean recede quickly into the distance. The eye is pulled rapidly and dramatically into a very deep space. The position of the sun rays reinforces the diagonal movement.

Notice the back of this quilt (Plate II-9) also shows depth. The Storm at Sea blocks gradually decrease in size and create depth. We also see the illusion of motion because of the Storm at Sea blocks.

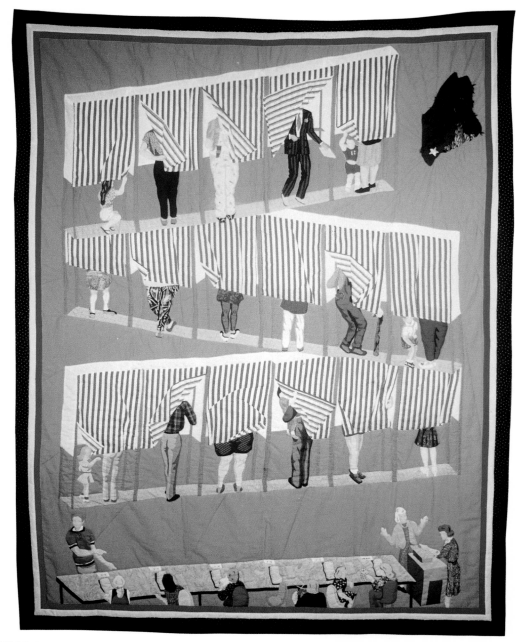

Plate II-10. LEGS GO OUT TO VOTE, 1994, 75" x 87", Marjorie B. Hansen, Windham, Maine. Marjorie used hand-piecing and hand appliqué to create a quilt that shows depth by the use of diagonal recession. Photo by Marjorie B. Hansen.

Though its artist was not trying for the illusion of great distance, the quilt LEGS GO OUT TO VOTE by Marjorie B. Hansen, shows the same diagonal recession (Plate II-10). The voting curtains recede sharply, with the white tops of the curtains emphasizing the diagonal. The registrar's tables recede to the right on a less acute angle.

Marjorie was inspired after a workshop on pictorial appliqué. As a ballot clerk, she took pictures of different legs in the voting booths. She is the one knitting in the foreground.

SPATIAL PUZZLES

Artists use various devices to give an illusion of depth or space. However, at times certain artists purposely ignore these practices to provide an unexpected image. A confusion of spatial relationships is intriguing because the viewer is confronted with a visual puzzle rather than a statement (Illustrations 2-1, 2-2, and 2-3).

M.C. Escher has produced many works that purposely employ this confusion of spatial relationships. His work is fascinating because, at first glance, the careful sketching and brilliant draftsmanship seem to present a perfectly straightforward scene. However, when you look again, suddenly the supposedly normal scene becomes a puzzling, impossible spatial situation.

Art is not a handicraft, it is the transmission of feeling the artist has experienced.
Leo Tolstoy

Illustration 2-1. Interweaving "V's" create a visual puzzle.

Look at Illustration 2-2 and 2-3. Can you really build this shape? Not in reality, but we as artists can build it — we can create what is not possible in reality.

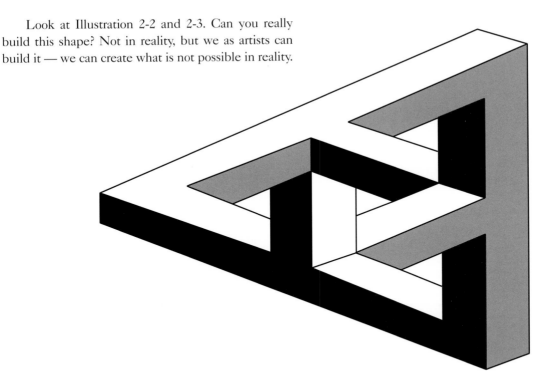

Illustration 2-2. The Impossible Triangle creates a visual puzzle.

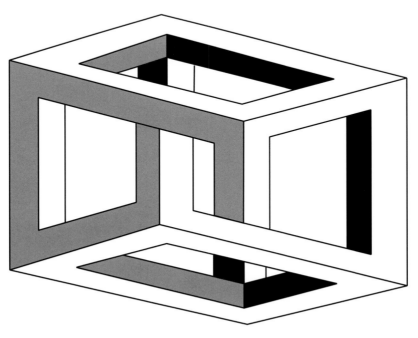

Illustration 2-3. The Impossible Square creates an intriguing puzzle.

Plate II-11. (KEEPING IT IN) PERSPECTIVE, 1994, 60" x 72", Pat Coulter, Williamsport, Pennsylvania. An M.C. Escher wood block print depicts a man holding such a cube inspired this visually intriguing quilt.

In (KEEPING IT IN) PERSPECTIVE, Pat Coulter creates a visually puzzling quilt (Plate II-11). We see boxes that cannot be interlocked in the fashion that they are. There is no way to explain this logically; we experience a strange visual paradox.

TRADITIONAL QUILT BLOCKS THAT ARE SPATIAL (VISUAL) PUZZLES

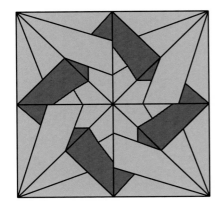

Tangled Stars 1244

Carpenter's Square 2580

Interlocked Squares 2618

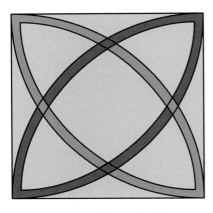

Love's Chain 4094

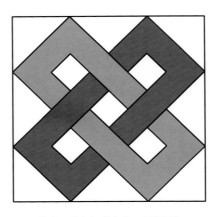

Friendship Links 4189**

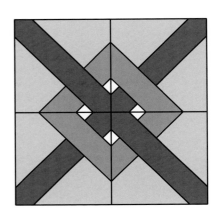

The Four Corners 4191

Double Square 4192

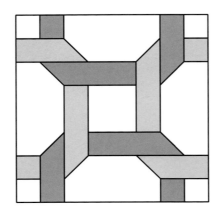

Plaited Block 4195

** indicates blocks in pattern section

Art is not a thing; it is a way.
Elbert Hubbard

PERSPECTIVE

"I try in my prints to testify that we live in a beautiful and orderly world, not in a chaos without norms, even though that is how it sometimes appears. My subjects are also often playful: I cannot refrain from demonstrating the non-sensicalness of some of what we take to be irrefutable certainties. It is, for example, a pleasure to deliberately mix together objects of two and three dimensions, surface and spatial relationships, and to make fun of gravity."

M.C. Escher

Perspective is a method of drawing the illusion of depth onto a flat surface. With this illusion we can create the appearance of a three-dimensional object on a flat surface. We can use this illusion very effectively in quilts; it is almost magical. Although it sounds complicated, it's really not. Perspective is drawing things as you really see them. To do this, we need to make a few observations.

The objects or shapes that we are drawing onto our flat surface, in real life, have depth and dimension. As we look at them and place them on our flat surface, we must always try to represent the depth. This makes the objects appear true and real. The shapes must appear to extend deeply into the illusional space of a quilt in order for the true magic of perspective to appear. We are creating the appearance of form, depth, and the natural play of light — all on the flat surface of our quilt.

Notice in the drawing of the two arrows that one of the arrows appears to have depth while the other appears flat. This is the magic of perspective.

Before we can add depth to our quilt, using the rules of perspective, we must draw out our scene. The foundation of all good drawings, no matter how beau-

DRAWING IN PERSPECTIVE

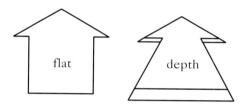

flat   depth

tifully shaded and colored, is correct perspective. If the perspective is not right, the quilt will look flat and out of proportion. Perspective can make or break a quilt that has all other elements presented perfectly.

Objects have different appearances when viewed from various positions. Because of this, we must establish a viewing point and stick with it for both the complete drawing and quilt. The viewing point is the position from which you view the subject. It is just like taking a snapshot; what you see through the viewfinder is what you will photograph. If you change position, you will get a different view of the same scene. We are going to capture one scene on our flat surface. When we draw this subject as it appears to the eye, we are then drawing in perspective.

The rules of perspective enable us to draw scenes or objects as they are perceived by the eye. There are several basic rules of perspective. As we study them, apply them to the objects in your home and the things around you every day. You will be amazed at what you will start to observe.

There are also several types of perspective. Linear perspective is one type; aerial perspective is another. We will look at both and apply them to our quiltmaking. Let's look first at linear perspective.

PERSPECTIVE

LINEAR PERSPECTIVE

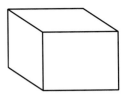

The main concept to consider in linear perspective is that all objects appear smaller the farther away they are from the viewing point. We discussed this when we looked at size as a depth cue. Remember the "monsters?" The space between them appeared to lessen as they became smaller with the distance. Take a look at the telephone poles in my neighborhood (Illustration 3-1). They appear to be smaller as they recede into the distant rolling hills. In reality, they are all the same size, but as I view them when I walk down the road, they seem to become smaller as they line the countryside.

Illustration 3-1. Telephone poles recede across the rolling hills of the author's middle Tennessee neighborhood. Photo by Karen Combs.

The poles appear to be receding toward a common point. That common point is the horizon. With the telephone poles, the farther away they appear, the closer to the horizon they will be. In the sky, the same applies — the closer to the horizon an object is, the more distant it appears.

TERMINOLOGY OF PERSPECTIVE

SUBJECT

Subject refers to the main focus in a drawing. It can be one item or many items, such as in a landscape.

As you begin your drawing, make sure that you have chosen a subject that you really want to work with or you will lose interest along the way. We all have experienced the feeling of excitement at the beginning of a project only to lose it as we actually work on it. UFOs (unfinished objects) are what they become. And we certainly don't need any more of those!

Be sure to pick your subject carefully and realize how much work there will be in producing a finished quilt.

PICTURE PLANE

The picture plane is an imaginary, transparent, flat plane between you and the drawn subject. In painting, the edges of the picture are the limits or the edges of the picture plane. In quilting, the borders are the edges of the picture plane.

When you are drawing, the surface of the paper is a two-dimensional plane. As you draw a three-dimensional object on paper, the drawn object becomes the picture plane. The illusion of depth and form has been produced on a flat surface.

Imagine, if you will, looking through a picture window. The scene within the edges of that picture window is the picture plane, the window itself is the surface. This is a simple but effective illustration of transferring the illusion of depth onto a flat surface.

An easy way to experience the value of the picture plane is to work on the glass of a picture window. Use a grease pencil and a 12" x 12" rotary square. Draw a square 12" x 12" on the window. The area within the square is the picture plane; the edges are the border.

Stand in one spot and, without moving your position, use the grease pencil to draw the outlines of what you see in the picture plane onto the window. Draw the outlines of cars, houses, trees, bushes, and whatever else you see. You have just drawn the 3-D depth and form on a flat surface. You have created on the window pane exactly what you would on your paper using an imaginary picture plane. It's fun! As you try a few different windows and views, you will really begin to understand this concept.

LINE OF VISION AND ELEVATION

Any object appears different when viewed from different angles.

For a scene to appear realistic, it must be viewed from the same viewpoint. This line of vision is what you see when you look straight ahead toward the horizon. If you look either to the left or the right, the line of vision will be changed. It must remain the same.

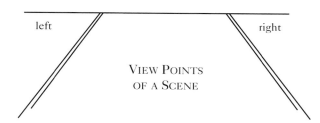

left   right

VIEW POINTS
OF A SCENE

As you were drawing on the picture window, you probably noticed that if you moved very much, the drawing became distorted and difficult to finish. Try moving to the left or to the right as you draw a scene and notice the difference.

The same is true if the height from which you view an object is changed. If the elevation is raised, the view of the object is downward. If the elevation is lowered, the view is upward. Once chosen, the elevation of view must be kept constant.

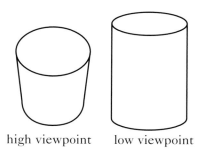

high viewpoint   low viewpoint

VIEWING ELEVATIONS

In Illustration 3-2, the elevation of view is very low, as if we were lying on the floor to view this scene. The view would be very different if we were to stand up and look down at the floor.

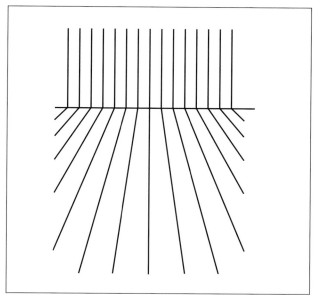

Illustration 3-2. Viewed from the floor.

HORIZON LINE OR EYE LEVEL

The horizon is the point where sea and sky or flat land and sky meet. This is the natural and true horizon.

The true horizon line is always at the level of your eyes and will change as you change the elevation of view. The higher you go, the higher the horizon line will be on the picture plane, showing more ground and less sky. The lower the elevation, the lower the horizon line will be and more sky will be seen. The position of the horizon line in our picture depends on the elevation from which we view the subject.

There are times when the true horizon line cannot be seen. A good example is when you are inside a room. The walls hide the true horizon. Although we can't see it, it is there. In order for the subject to be drawn correctly, the horizon must be kept in mind.

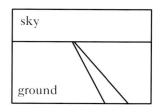

HIGHER ELEVATION

As you draw your scene, remember any object that is level and parallel to the ground plane, such as a table top or floor, will be affected by the horizon line.

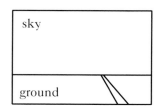

LOWER ELEVATION

DRAWING ONE-POINT PERSPECTIVE

Step 1. Draw the front of the cube, then draw two lines that angle back from the top of the cube until they cross.

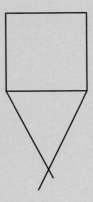

VANISHING POINT

Lines that are parallel to one another and level with the ground plane, such as furrows in a plowed field, appear to meet at the same point on the horizon line. This point is known as the vanishing point (Illustration 3-3).

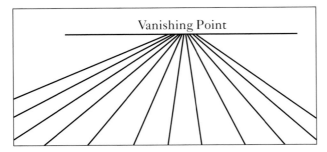

Illustration 3-3.

This point is very important to any perspective drawing. If the vanishing point is misplaced, the object in the drawing will be distorted. The vanishing point must be established accurately to draw any scene correctly.

Step 2. Where the lines cross, draw a horizontal line parallel to the top of the square. This is the horizon line. Next, place a dot where the three lines cross. This is the vanishing point.

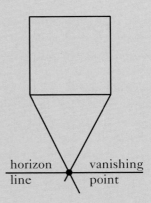

horizon line   vanishing point

TYPES
OF LINEAR
PERSPECTIVE

The three types of linear perspective used most often are one-point, two-point, and three-point perspective. Let's look at each.

ONE-POINT PERSPECTIVE

In one-point perspective, the height and width of an object are always parallel to the picture plane.

Step 3. Draw a parallel line two-thirds of the way from the horizon line to the top of the square. This line establishes the bottom surface of a cube drawn in perfect one-point perspective.

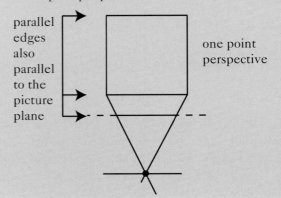

parallel edges also parallel to the picture plane

one point perspective

TO FIND INSIDE EDGES

Step 4. Starting with the square, establish the top of the box by extending lines from the top left and right corners to the vanishing point.

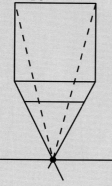

Step 5. Draw vertical lines down from the back left and right corners of the line drawn to form the top of the cube. The width of the back wall is now established. This makes the side walls.

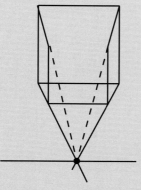

Step 6. Draw a horizontal line from the back left corner to the right one. This gives us the width of the back wall in true one-point perspective. Erase any unneeded lines.

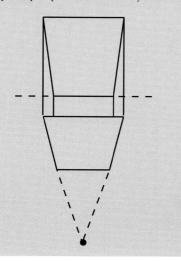

When you draw a cube above the horizon line, it gives the cube the illusion of flying.

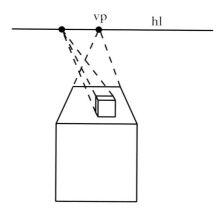

If a cube is drawn below the horizon line, it will appear to be lying on the ground. Using a different vanishing point, place a small cube on the top of the cube. See how easily you can draw different cubes using different vanishing points and the horizon line as a guide.

The boxes below are drawn in different sizes and positions using the same perspective point. Notice the height and the width of the boxes are always parallel to the picture plane.

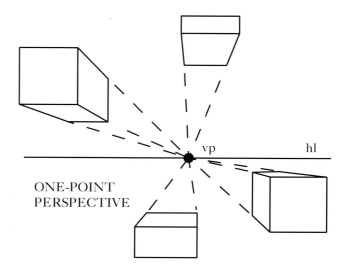

ONE-POINT PERSPECTIVE

Plate III-1. FANTASTIC VIEW, 1990, 80" x 80", Wendy Hill, Nevada City, California. Wendy used a CAD program to skew and distort her fans. She printed out the blocks and used the printout for her templates. She based her work on a one-point perspective within the computer program. Photo by Wendy Hill.

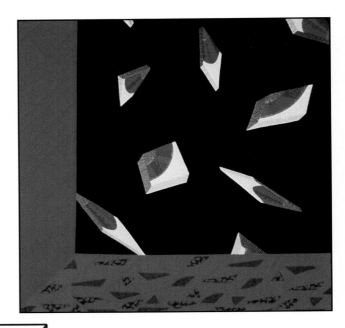

Illustration 3-4.

FANTASTIC VIEW by Wendy Hill is a perfect example of one-point perspective used in a quilt (Plate III-1). Wendy used different vanishing points to create the different fan blocks.

Illustration 3-4 is another good example of one-point perspective. Notice how the sides of the boxes recede toward the vanishing point in the center.

Plate III-2. IN DEPTH, 1987, 73" x 80", Bobbie Fuhrmann, Lancaster, New York. Bobbie used a variation of the Stepping Stones quilt block and incorporated one-point perspective to set the blocks together. Photo by AQS.

Illustration 3-5.

The quilt IN DEPTH by Bobbie Fuhrmann is an original interpretation of the traditional quilt block, Stepping Stones (Illustration 3-5). Bobbie likes to find innovative ways to use traditional patterns in her quilts.

Bobbie used one-point perspective in setting the blocks together. This quilt was pieced and quilted by hand and it was a very difficult quilt to piece because the center of the quilt is slightly off-center. This made every piece in the "sides and top" of the quilt a different size. Bobbie made a full-size drawing of the quilt and cut out the separate templates for each piece in those sections, making sure that a piece didn't get turned sideways or upside down when she was cutting or piecing it. Everything was asymmetrical and would fit only one way!

PROPORTIONS AND DIVISIONS

DRAWING QUILT BLOCKS IN PERSPECTIVE

Step 1. To find the center of a square, draw diagonal lines from corner to corner. The point where they cross is the true center.

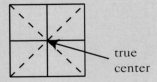

true center

Step 2. In perspective, the square is at an angle, but you can use the same method to find the perspective center.

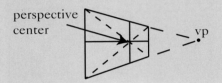

perspective center

vp

UPRIGHT OBJECTS AND STANDING QUILT BLOCKS

Any object that is equally spaced apart like fence posts, railroad ties, telephone poles, and even "standing quilt blocks," can be drawn correctly by using the following example of proportional division.

After trying the example in the book, practice drawing some examples of your own. The more you practice, the better you will be at judging your drawings. Most of the time, you will be measuring and drawing these objects by eye and with practice, you will be right most of the time. If something does not look quite right, the knowledge of perspective and the methods of proportional division will be helpful in correcting the error.

Now, try drawing a quilt block.

DRAWING UPRIGHT OBJECTS

Step 1. Draw a line to make the left edge of the block. Stretch a line from the top and bottom of the quilt block until they cross. Place a vanishing point where they cross. Then, by eye, draw the right edge of the quilt block.

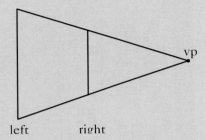

left   right

Step 2. Find the perspective center using the method just learned. Then draw a line through the center to the vanishing point.

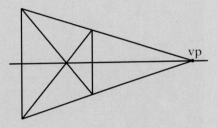

vp

Step 3. Draw a line from the top of the quilt block through the center point. Where this line touches the bottom line is the location for the next quilt block.

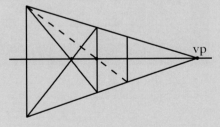

vp

Step 4. Repeat as often as needed to create the rest of the quilt blocks.

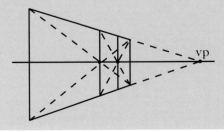

vp

PUTTING QUILT BLOCKS IN PERSPECTIVE

Once the quilt blocks are drawn, it's time to divide the area and draw in some quilt patterns.

Step 5. You can use this method to divide the area into rectangles.

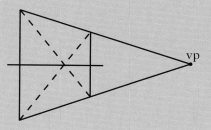

Step 6. Or, divide the quilt block into squares.

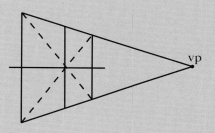

Step 7. Once you have divided the area, you can draw in a quilt block. Use this method to draw a four-patch quilt block like Broken Dishes.

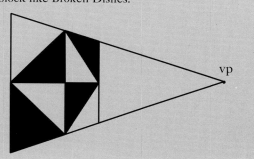

TWO-POINT PERSPECTIVE

In two-point perspective, we are viewing a cube at an angle, not head-on as with one-point perspective. Also in two-point only the height is parallel to the picture plane. Because there are two vanishing lines instead of one, the sides recede into the depth of the picture plane.

These vanishing points will be placed on the horizon line as they were for one-point perspective. As the vanishing points move farther apart, we see more of each side. Notice that the sides of the cube appear smaller as they recede into the depth of the picture.

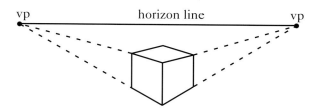

As the two points move closer together, we see less of one side than the other.

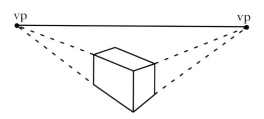

As with one-point perspective, once the viewing point has been established, it must remain constant.

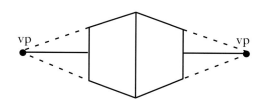

DRAWING TWO-POINT PERSPECTIVE

Step 1. Draw a line. This is the corner of your cube. Draw it as long as you wish it to be.

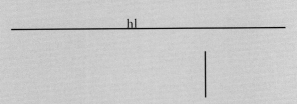

Step 2. Stretch the top and bottom lines from the left side of the cube to the horizon line. Where the lines cross this line, place a vanishing point. Draw a vertical line. This establishes the back edge of the cube.

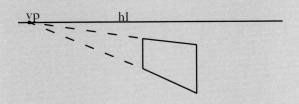

Step 3. Stretch the top and bottom lines from the right side of the cube to the horizon line. Again, where they cross, place a vanishing point.
Draw a vertical line on the right side to establish the right back edge of the cube.

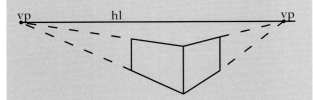

Step 4. To draw the top of the cube, draw two top lines using the vanishing points. The top will be automatically created at the point where these two lines cross at the back of the cube.

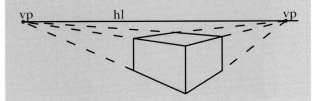

TO FIND THE "INSIDE" EDGES

Step 5. Using the cube just drawn, stretch a line from the right back corner to the left vanishing point.

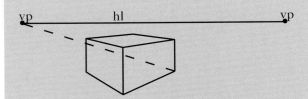

Step 6. Draw a vertical line down from the back top corner. Where this line touches the line just drawn will create the back side wall.

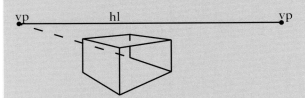

Step 7. Stretch a line from the left corner to the right vanishing point. Where this line touches the line just drawn will create the back wall. Erase any unneeded lines.

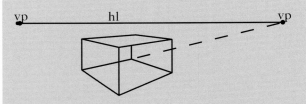

Step 8. Using one-point perspective, draw a small cube inside this one. You have now combined one- and two-point perspective.

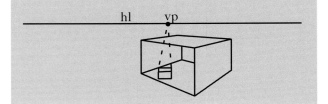

You can see how easily you can combine one- and two-point persective in a drawing, even using the same vanishing points. Notice how the two-point perspective cubes differ in appearance. When placed at different elevations, they will look quite distinct.

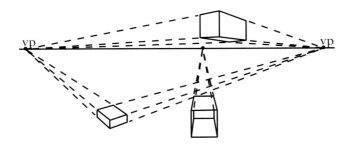

Practice drawing cubes at different elevations and try mixing one- and two-point perspectives in the same drawings. This combination is very easy to do.

HOUSES

Let's draw a schoolhouse quilt block in two-point perspective.

DRAWING A HOUSE

Step 1. Draw the Schoolhouse block in two-point perspective. Refer to the two-point exercises if needed.

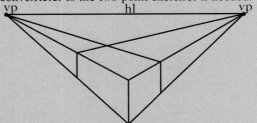

Step 2. Let's give it a roof. To find the point of the roof, find the perspective center of the ends of the house. Draw vertical lines from the centers and stretch them above the walls.

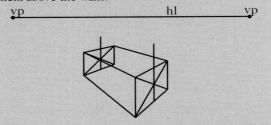

Step 3. Draw a line from the roof height to the left vanishing point.

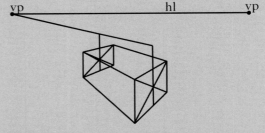

Step 4. Draw a line from the roof point to the front and back corners.

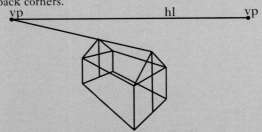

Step 5. Erase unneeded lines and you now have a Schoolhouse drawn in perfect perspective.

DIVIDING OF AREAS

If we need to divide an area, such as for a floor or a horizontal quilt block, the method is easy to do.

Step 1. This area has been drawn in two-point perspective.

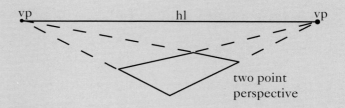

Step 2. Place a horizontal line at the bottom of the area and divide into equal portions — in this case five. However, you can divide the area into whatever number you wish.

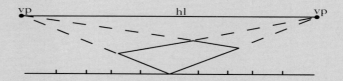

Step 3. Draw a diagonal line from each division to the right vanishing point. Repeat for the left vanishing point.

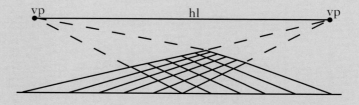

Step 4. Erase unneeded lines and draw a quilt block in the newly created grid. In this case, Lady of the Lake.

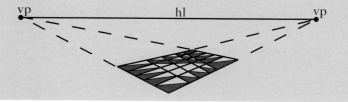

THREE-POINT PERSPECTIVE

In three-point perspective, a third vanishing point is added either above or below the object being drawn. This is an exciting perspective to use and it can give a dramatic effect to our quilts.

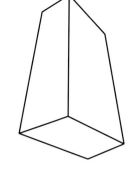

A general rule of perspective is that all vertical lines are kept truly vertical unless three-point perspective is used. Let's draw a building using three-point perspective. First we will draw it as if we are looking down at it.

Practice, if desired, in the space below.

DRAWING THREE-POINT PERSPECTIVE

Step 1. Using two-point perspective, establish the corner of the box or building that is closest to you. Draw that vertical line, then establish the angles of the sides by drawing in the top and bottom guidelines.

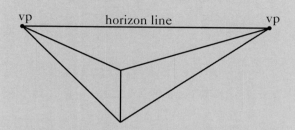

Step 2. By eye, establish the desired width of each side by placing dots on the bottom lines. Place a dot on the guideline above the bottom left dot.

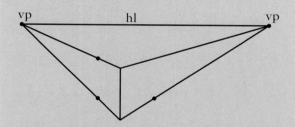

Step 3. Extend a line downward from the center vertical line. Then draw a line from the top left dot, through the bottom left dot, and extend the line until it crosses extended vertical. The point at which these two lines cross is the vanishing point.

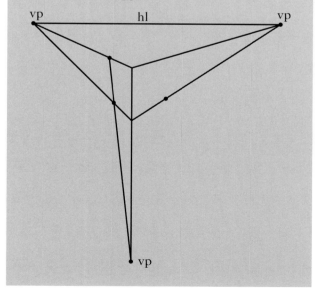

STEP BY STEP INSTRUCTIONS

Step 4. Draw a line through the right dot, down to the third vanishing point and up through the top line. You now have the proper angles for the sides of the building. Finish by drawing in the roof of the building, using the right and left vanishing points.

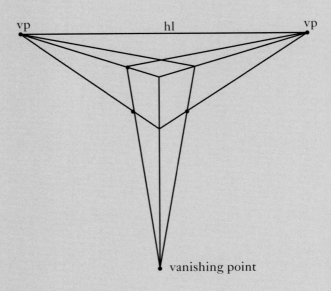

Step 5. Now practice drawing the same building looking up at it (as seen in the illustration on previous page).

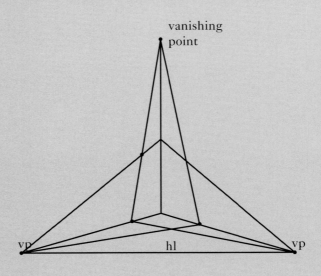

Plate III-3. QUILTS IN SPACE, 1990, 51" x 46", Ellen Anne Eddy, Chicago, Illinois. This quilt was done as a color study in three-point perspective. Photo by Ellen Anne Eddy.

Plate III-4. Detail of QUILTS IN SPACE.

QUILTS IN SPACE by Ellen Anne Eddy uses three-point perspective to create a dramatic quilt (Plates III-3 and III-4). It was pieced and quilted by machine and is a wonderful example of three-point perspective, using the traditional quilt block Ohio Star.

AERIAL PERSPECTIVE

Aerial perspective is the representation of space by gradations of color that parallel the effect produced by various densities of air on the appearance of objects. Yikes! Let me see if I can put that more simply. The farther away objects are, the more bluish they will seem to be, and their images will be fuzzy. We will examine this concept in detail in Chapters 7 and 8.

Aerial perspective is seen as the distant hills appear bluish in comparison to the green hills in the foreground.

HOW DO YOU TRANSLATE AN IDEA INTO A QUILT?

The best way to approach making a quilt is to draw it full size. You can get trash paper from art supply stores and tape pieces together to get the correct size. Trash paper in a large roll is fairly inexpensive. You could also draw a scene on a regular sheet of paper and project it with an overhead projector onto a full-size trash paper pattern.

When you are satisfied with the full-size drawing, darken all the lines with a fine-line black marker. You may even want to shade in the design with colored pencils to help identify design elements.

Place the drawing on a table and tape it down; a light table will be helpful.

You can easily make a light table by removing leaves from your dining room table. Place a lamp under the table and a sheet of plexiglass on the table where the leaves were. Voilà, a light table.

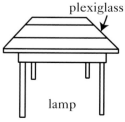

Tape a piece of freezer paper, paper side up, over the drawing. For larger drawings, work one section at a time or tape several pieces of freezer paper together. Trace all lines onto the freezer paper, using a ruler to keep the lines straight. This drawing will be used to make the templates, so it needs to be accurate.

Number each piece. You need to do this to keep the pieces straight as you sew them together. It may help to identify the pieces by a code; such as background pieces: B1, B2, B3, house pieces: H1, H2, H3, etc.

Cut apart the freezer paper drawing, working one section at a time to avoid confusion and to avoid losing small pieces. These freezer paper pieces are your templates. Use a rotary cutter with an old blade for cutting the paper apart. Paper dulls your cutter, so don't use a new blade.

With a hot, dry iron, press the freezer paper templates to the back of your fabric. Try to keep the grain line consistent with the edge of your quilt. You may want to mark grain lines on the freezer paper as you draw. With a ruler and rotary cutter, cut the fabric pieces, adding a ¼" seam allowance as you cut.

Start sewing the small inner pieces first. Add the units together as you build the design. Do not remove the paper until you have sewn all the pieces in a section. Press with a dry iron.

When you are finished, remove the paper and carefully press with a steam iron, making sure not to stretch the piece out of shape.

Cut fabric pieces, adding ¼" seam allowance, using a ruler and a rotary cutter. Photo by Gail Burrow.

SKETCHBOOK These figures include some sketches I have drawn using various perspectives. Use the sketches to give you some ideas for combining perspective and traditional quilt blocks.

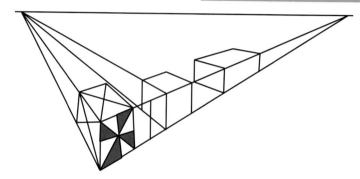

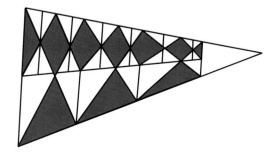

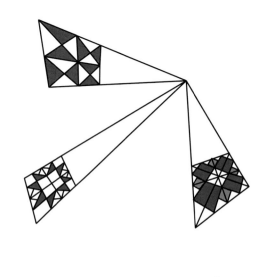

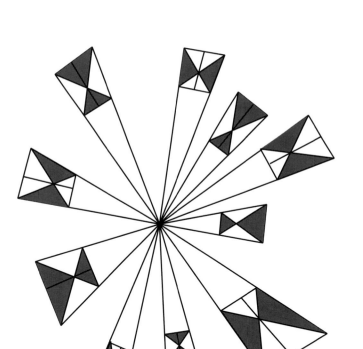

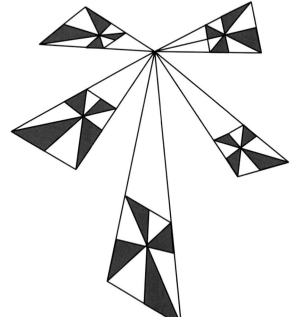

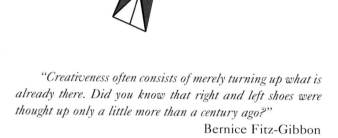

"Creativeness often consists of merely turning up what is already there. Did you know that right and left shoes were thought up only a little more than a century ago?"
Bernice Fitz-Gibbon

Optical Illusions for Quilters

CHAPTER 4

ISOMETRIC PERSPECTIVE

See first that the design is wise and just; that ascertained, pursue it resolutely; do not for one repulse forgo the purpose that you resolved to effect.

William Shakespeare

In contrast to one-point and two-point perspective, isometric perspective is most commonly found in the Eastern, Chinese, Japanese, Indian, and Islamic art. This is a type of linear perspective without a vanishing point. We will not see objects getting smaller in the distance as they do with a vanishing point.

Isometric perspective favors straight edges and geometric forms. It is an excellent method for quilters to use to achieve an illusion of depth.

Look at the two cubes in Illustration 4-1. Cube A is drawn with a vanishing point, while cube B is drawn in isometric perspective. They have a totally different look although each has the illusion of depth.

The idea of viewpoint is treated differently in isometric perspective as well. There is no single viewpoint as in one-point perspective. Instead, the viewer floats above the scene, able to see everywhere. The space appears infinite as the eye moves up, down, and across. However, the image is also flatter. Isometric

perspective seems to move shapes sideways in a zigzag pattern rather than into the picture.

This flatter space allows for an easy interaction between the flat surface of a quilt or drawing and the three-dimensional feeling of space. It constantly recognizes the flatness of the picture and returns the eye to the picture plane and the rhythms moving across it.

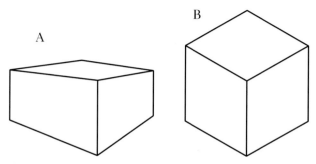

Illustration 4-1. The cube on the left is drawn in one-point perspective, the one on the right in isometric perspective.

Plate IV-1. HARLEQUIN CUBE, 1993, 28" x 31", Karen Combs, Columbia, Tennessee. Isometric perspective gives the illusion of depth while recognizing the flatness of the picture. The pattern for this quilt is included in the pattern section. Photo by Charles R. Lynch, American Quilter's Society.

Consequently, the sense of isometric perspective has been a preferred tool of many modern artists working in ways that emphasize surface over deep space. The magical quality of isometric perspective that allows near and far to alternate is gracefully maximized in my quilt, HARLEQUIN CUBE (Plate IV-1). The image seems both deep and strangely flat, front and center reverse, and forms are drawn toward the front as they move simultaneously toward the back.

Isometric perspective is also used by architects. It is a useful method for presenting an overview of sizes and positions of rooms, corridors, and so forth. The isometric perspective is preferred by architects because it distorts the space less than a vanishing point perspective.

Look again at the cubes in Illustration 4-1. An isometrically drawn cube keeps its edges parallel. The parallel lines do not become converging lines as in one-point perspective.

This principle works well for quilters. Unlike in one-point perspective, single templates can be used, rather than multiple templates. I like to use this method, because after I've sketched out an idea I like, I can rotary cut my pieces all at once.

Let's explore the wonderful world of isometric perspective, one of my favorite illusions.

BABY BLOCKS AND A LIGHT SOURCE

You may be familiar with isometric perspective without even realizing it. The traditional Baby Blocks or Tumbling Blocks is based on isometric perspective.

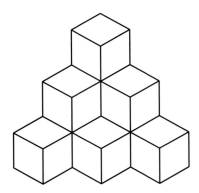

Illustration 4-2.

Tumbling Blocks, Illustration 4-2, is based on a 60° diamond. The piecing unit is composed of 12 diamonds. If care is taken with value placement, the tumbling block pattern will be created (Illustration 4-3). However, as in Ilustration 4-4, you can create a six-pointed star if the value is placed in a different position.

To create the look of depth in Tumbling Blocks, a dark fabric is needed on one side, medium on another, and light on the third side. Imagine a light source shining down on the block. The light side will always be on the top of the block. The placement of the medium and dark will depend on whether the light source is to the left or to the right of our block.

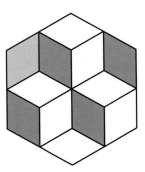

Illustration 4-3. This piecing unit is composed of twelve 60° diamonds.

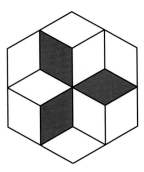

Illustration 4-4. If the value is not properly placed, the depth will not show.

In Illustration 4-5, the light source is slightly to the right of the block. This results in the medium value on the right side of the block and the darkest value on the left side of the block. If the light source is placed to the left, the medium and dark values will be reversed.

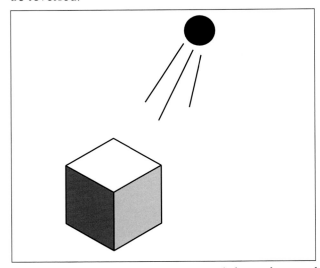

Illustration 4-5. The light source creates a light, medium, and dark side to the cube.

Optical Illusions for Quilters

Plate IV-2. CAN YOU SEE THE DIAMONDS? 1993, 82" x 89", Mary Beth Bellah, Charlottesville, Virginia. This design was created by Mary Beth's desire to use four colors in a three color unit block. Photo by Mary Beth Bellah.

The light source can be anywhere you want, even on the bottom. Just remember to be consistent on your value placement. In CAN YOU SEE THE DIAMONDS? Mary Beth Bellah kept the values in the same placement! However, by adding a fourth color to her quilt, she creates an interwoven tumbling block pattern (Plate IV-2).

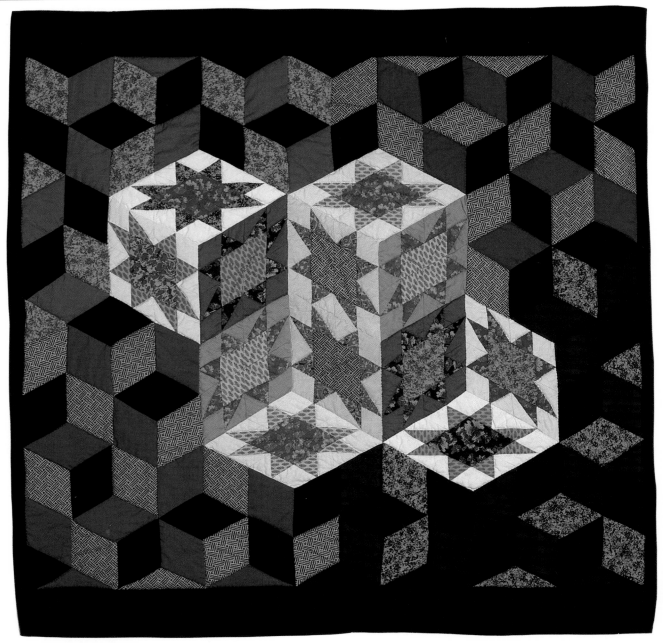

Plate IV-3. TUMBLED STARS, 1994, 36" x 36", Karen Combs. Different value placement of the tumbling blocks in the background creates an intriguing visual and spatial illusion. Photo by Charles R. Lynch, American Quilter's Society.

Of course, once you know the rules, it's fun to stretch them. I like to play with rules and see what I can do. Look at the background of TUMBLED STARS (Plate IV-3). I mixed up the value placement of the diamonds and discovered an interesting variation.

Sometimes you can see a single baby block in the background and sometimes a double block appears. If you pick out any one dark patch, you will see that only medium and light diamonds are placed next to it. You will also notice every light diamond has only dark and medium diamonds next to it.

Optical Illusions for Quilters

Keeping it all straight may seem mind-boggling, but it is relatively easy. Only diamonds were used in the background. I drew my design and developed the background on my design wall, one section at a time. By mixing up the background, the eye has more to look at and wonderful spatial puzzles are created.

TUMBLED STARS is based on a design by Victor Vasarely. I put patchwork stars in the larger tumbling blocks for a wonderful 3-D effect. Ahead in the chapter, we'll learn how to create the 3-D patchwork.

DEVELOPING WORK HABITS/DESIGN WALL

While working on TUMBLED STARS, I worked on the value placement before anything was sewn. Working on a design wall to choose my color placement, I discovered I had to discard some pieces and substitute others. Don't be reluctant to discard a few pieces of fabric. It's hard to "waste" a patch, but that is why we have our fabric stashes. Fabric is our palette. Use it! When I was satisfied with the look of an area, it was sewn together.

Quilters have various methods of putting their work on a wall. Some use a giant cork board, others pin directly into the wall or pin to wallpaper, some put up a 4'x8' piece of Celotex wallboard. I use a large piece of fleece that is tacked to my wall from the ceiling to the floor.

Some of my friends have come up with other interesting creations for their design walls. One friend uses the back of an old plastic tablecloth; it's fuzzy and fabric sticks to it. Another friend uses a large piece of batting tacked to the wall. Still another friend uses a 4-foot square foam insulation board covered with flannel. She even put a ribbon on the top of it and hangs it right on the wall.

Before I had a sewing room of my own, I used a corner of our family room. I could not put up a perma-nent design wall, so a temporary one was created. There was only one place large enough for a design wall — the sliding glass door. And that's what I used. A large piece of flannel was taped to the glass. I could fold it up when I was done, when company was coming, or when the weather got nice and we wanted to use the door.

Why use a design wall? It is better to view your work straight on rather than looking down at it on the floor. You get a better view point and can really see if the design is working. It is also great if you have a bad back — no more bending up and down.

Using a reducing glass (Illustration 4-6) gives me a little better idea what the quilt will look like when it is sewn together.

Illustration 4-6. View through a reducing glass. Photo by Gail Burrow.

COLOR AND VALUE

Once you have a block drawn that pleases you, it's time to choose the color and value of the block. I like to use my newly created blocks in settings that have a 3-D look, such as in HARLEQUIN CUBE (Plate IV-1). There are a few guidelines that are helpful in creating the illusion of depth.

Remember, your block needs a light side, a medium side, and a dark side. Imagine the position of your light source and place the values on the appropriate sides. Shade in the values on your drawing with pencil. Sketch your block in several different value placements until you are satisfied. Now, pick out some colors.

Warm colors like red, yellow, and orange, advance toward your eye and cool colors like blue, green, and purple, retreat away from your eye. You can use this technique to your advantage with your cubes. In HARLEQUIN CUBE, I used cool colors on the outside of the block to retreat away from the eye and used warm colors on the inside of the cube to come toward the eye. Using color in this way will enhance the 3-D illusion. In Chapter Seven, this is discussed in detail.

For the background color, I like to use either a very dark or a very light, subtle print. Black works very well as does a "sky" fabric. I never use a busy print for the background; it is too distracting and will take away from the 3-D blocks.

I find in 3-D patchwork it is helpful for each cube to stay within a single color family. If your cube is blue, use several light blues on one side, several medium blues on a second side, and several dark blues on the third side. Trying to use several different colors within a single cube can be distracting. When choosing fabric, don't make it too busy. Your eye will see the busyness of the fabric and not the depth. Look at TUMBLED STARS (Plate IV-3) and see how the correct use of value and color enhances the illusion of depth.

3-D DESIGN

Now that we know a bit about value placement, let's combine traditional quilt blocks and 3-D blocks.

DESIGNING

First, select a patchwork block you want to work with. For ease of construction, I like to use blocks that use only squares, and half-square triangles (Illustration 4-7).

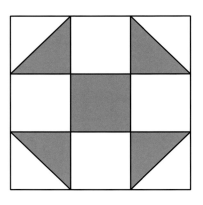

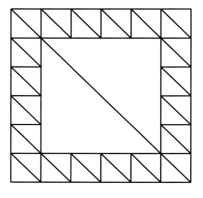

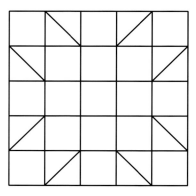

Illustration 4-7. Squares and half-square triangles are used to create these quilt blocks.

Look through patchwork block books such as Jinny Beyers' *Quilter's Album of Blocks and Borders* or Shirley Liby's *Exploring Four-Patch* and *Designing with Nine-Patch*. You will need to know the block's divisions or what "patch" the block is as you draw the blocks, so books that show divisions are helpful.

After selecting the block you want to use, you'll need equilateral triangle graph paper. This paper is available at most quilt shops or you can find it at a drafting supply store. I use this paper to design all my 3-D blocks based on isometric perspective.

Draw a block on triangle graph paper just as you would on square graph paper. If your block has three divisions, draw your grid three by three; if it has four divisions, draw it four by four. Any patch block will work, from a simple four-patch to a seven-patch.

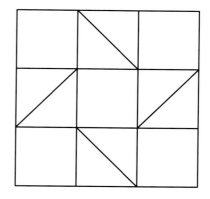

Illustration 4-8a. Friendship Star quilt block drawn in a Nine-Patch grid.

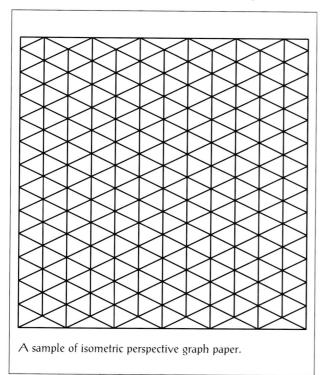

A sample of isometric perspective graph paper.

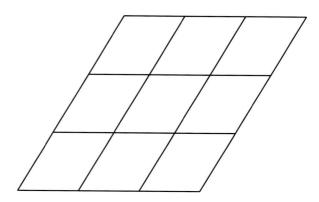

Illustration 4-8b. Nine-Patch grid drawn on isometric graph paper.

After you draw the grid, it's time to fill it in. Let's take the patchwork block Friendship Star and draw it in our new grid (Illustrations 4-8a, 4-8b, and 4-8c).

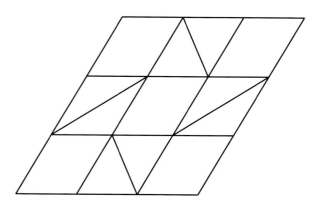

Illustration 4-8c. Friendship Star drawn in a Nine-Patch grid on isometric graph paper.

For more practice, look at the sample blocks below and try to fill in the grid. It may take a few tries to think in this "sideways" grid, but keep trying.

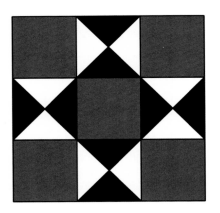

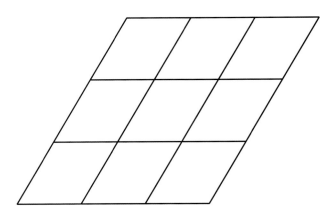

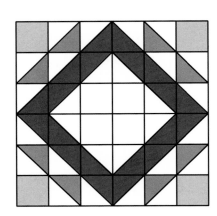

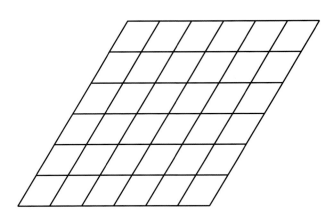

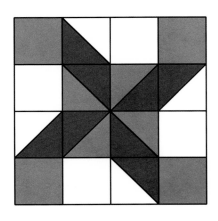

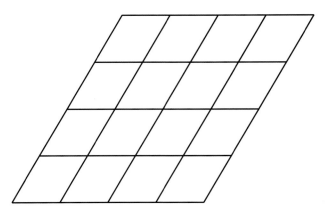

Optical Illusions for Quilters

Plate IV-4. ATTIC WINDOWS FROM A DIFFERENT ANGLE, 1993, 48" x 54", Karen Combs. Attic Windows set in a 60° angle instead of a 45° create an entirely different look.

After you have drawn the sample blocks, select a few from a quilt block book and practice on graph paper. Notice in my quilt ATTIC WINDOWS FROM A DIFFERENT ANGLE (Plate IV-4), all the quilt blocks inserted in the attic window settings are four-patches.

Plate IV-5. CUBE FANTASY I, 1988, 34" x 34", Wendy Hill, Nevada City, California. Wendy was inspired in general by the 3-D work of Jeff Gutcheon, however, the application of the idea was entirely her own. Photo by James, Image Maker Studio.

Wendy Hill, in CUBE FANTASY I, uses a giant Bear's Paw on the outside of the cube and a checkerboard on the inside walls and floor of the cube (Plate IV-5). In this quilt, you have an interesting effect of a floating cube with a hollow inside.

Notice on the sample blocks below where the cubes are used. You can create many patchwork blocks using just these basic shapes. The numbers on the shapes correspond to the templates in the project section on page 159.

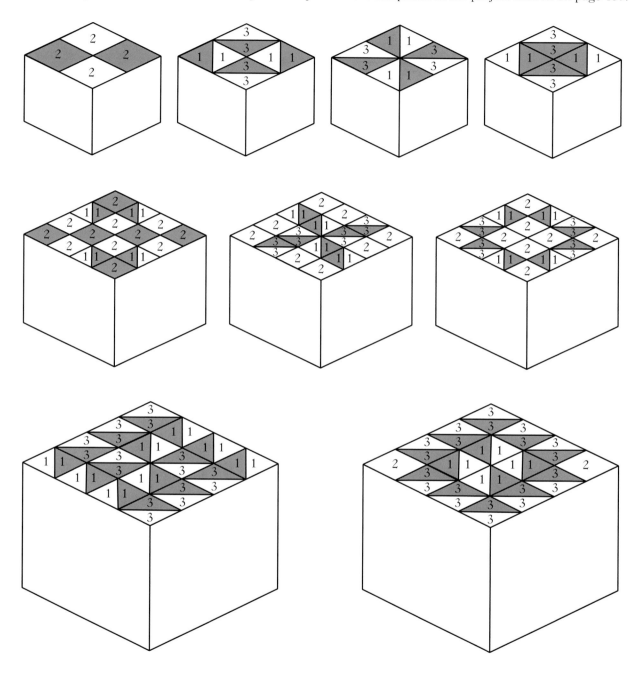

CUTTING Once you have the block drawn and have selected fabrics, it's time to cut out the pieces. I've added general cutting and piecing instructions using templates in the project section on pages 157 – 159.

SEWING You can put these cubes together in some interesting settings. If you want all the cubes to fit together, as in a tumbling blocks setting, use blocks that all have the same grid number.

If you design a 3" x 3" gridded cube, keep all the other cubes at that grid.

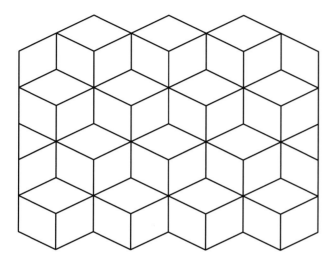

A Tumbling Blocks setting.

If you use blocks with different grids, they will stack up or stack out. They will not fit together very well. You can use this knowledge to your advantage if you want to create a stacked-up setting

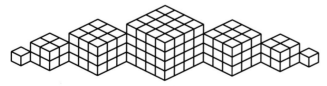

Blocks of different grids side by side.

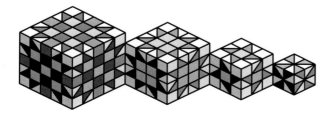

Blocks of different grids look like stair steps.

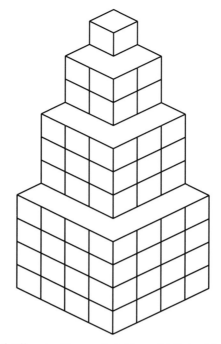

Blocks of different grids can stack like a child's toy blocks.

BACKGROUND In most cases, you can appliqué your cube set onto the background fabric. When appliquéing, always use a thread that matches what you are sewing down, not the background.

A single Shoo Fly 3-D cube makes a dramatic wallhanging.

SKETCHBOOK

Here are some sketches to inspire you and give you some ideas where you can use 3-D design; use these blocks together in a quilt or separately on clothing.

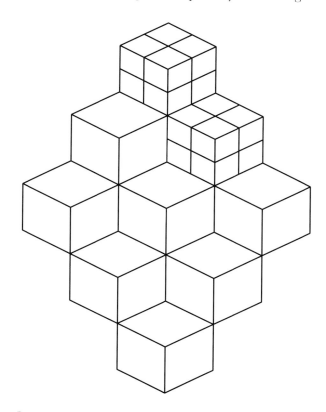

Optional settings for 3-D patchwork.

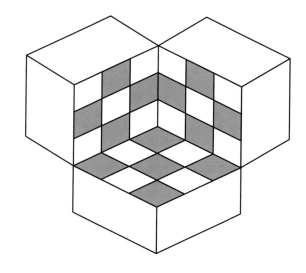

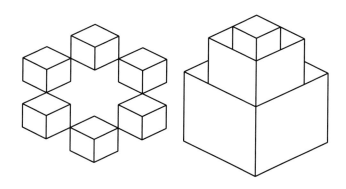

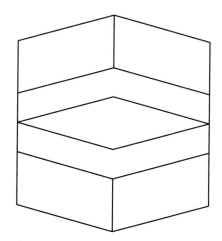

More ideas for 3-D patchwork.

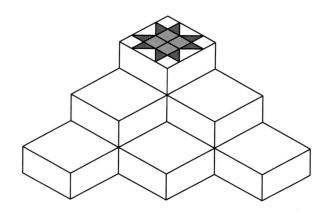

CHAPTER 5

MOTION AS AN ILLUSION

It is often said that a photograph or drawing of a moving object shows movement, but that motion is an illusion. The motion that is sensed in a photograph or pictorial quilt isn't really motion at all. Pick up a photograph and shake it; the shapes and colors do not rattle around. Everything is fixed in place. But we still speak of "movement."

Illustration 5-1. This galloping horse seems to be galloping backward.

Illustration courtesy of CorelDRAW.

Only movies or TV can show us "moving pictures." In paintings or drawings that are static images, any feeling of motion or change is always a suggestion or an illusion. This illusion, however, has intrigued artists of many time periods and countries.

In Illustration 5-1, the artist has accurately captured the image of a horse galloping forward, but the clip art does not show forward motion at all. Rather, the horse seems to be galloping backward.

What, then, is the relationship between moving objects and pictorial movement? One way to find out is to look at how artists control and organize the elements of a composition to make motion appear on a still page.

Change and movement are basic characteristics of existence. Our world is a world of movement. Almost every aspect of life involves constant change. We cannot sit or stand motionless for more than a few moments; even in sleep we turn and change position. But if we could stop our body movements, the world about us would continue to change. Thus, motion is an important consideration in art.

The quilts in Plates V-1 and V-2 have many visual differences, but both present a feeling of motion.

Optical Illusions for Quilters

Plate V-1. PRIMAL II, 1989, 68" x 51", Jean Neblett, San Francisco, California. The complexity is created when bisecting pattern and the uninterrupted movement crosses boundaries. Photo by David Belda.

In the quilt PRIMAL II by Jean Neblett, our eyes dart rapidly around the surface, following the complicated pattern of fabric, color, and quilting lines (Plate V-1). This is an example of Abstract Expressionism, an apt description for we can sense the physical activity of the artist in creating the quilt. This style has movement and dynamic excitement as primary goals. Jean machine pieced and machine quilted this complex quilt. She used curved piecing with cut-throughs to create motion.

Plate V-2. ENTROPY IS INCREASING IN MY UNIVERSE, 1996, 58" x 64", Barbara Barrick McKie, Lyme, Connecticut. Barbara created her first op-art quilt in 1975. She machined pieced, machine appliquéd, and machine quilted this marvelous quilt. Photo by Barbara Barrick McKie.

    ENTROPY IS INCREASING IN MY UNIVERSE by Barbara Barrick McKie shows a different technique (Plate V-2). It is a very controlled, repetitive pattern of definite, hard-edged lines. But when we stare at it, the edges begin to blur and the lines begin to "swim," as the areas vibrate. This type of art is called "Op-Art," images that give optical illusions of movement in static images.

    Two quilts quite dissimilar in style achieve the same goal — an illusion of motion.

ANTICIPATED
MOTION

Much of the implication of movement present in art is caused by our memory and experience. We recognize temporary, unstable body positions and realize that change must be imminent (Illustration 5-2).

Illustration 5-2. A temporary body position indicates change is imminent.

You can't get all the way just on facts. To get to a wonderful place you have to let your imagination take you the last leg.

Garrison Keillor
Prairie Home Companion, 1986

Illustration courtesy of CorelDRAW.

Plate V-3. TAPPING IN THE ATTIC, 1992, 80" x 68", Carol Goddu, Ontario, Canada. Carol used the traditional attic window pattern as a setting for the pictorial appliqué. An excellent example of anticipated motion. Photo by Richard Walker.

We can immediately "see" the action shown in TAPPING IN THE ATTIC by Carol Goddu (Plate V-3). The dancers are in poses that we recognize as momentary, and we anticipate the change that is imminent. The dancer kicking up her leg will obviously not be in this position for more than a moment; we anticipate her taking her next step.

Carol was inspired by photographs of tap dancers, especially those in Bob Fosse's Broadway productions.

In this process called "kinesthetic empathy," we tend to recreate unconsciously in our own bodies the actions we observe. We actually "feel" in our muscles the exertions of the athlete or dancer. We stretch, push, or lean, even though we are only watching. This involuntary reaction also applies to static images in art, where it can enhance the feeling of movement.

ANTICIPATED MOTION QUILT BLOCKS

I've selected a few pictorial quilt blocks that show anticipated motion. You can see each animal has been captured in a position that will "change" in a moment, thus giving the appearance of motion. When creating a pictorial quilt, put some of your figures in positions that appear to be "frozen." It will give your quilt interest and motion.

TRADITIONAL QUILT BLOCKS THAT SHOW ANTICIPATED MOTION

Wild Cat 937.6

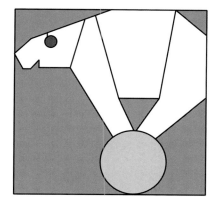
Polar Bear 939.2

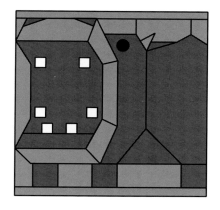
Hippopotamus 939.6

My quilts are sort of a daydream put down with pieces of cloth.

Adabelle Dremann

Plate V-4. CUERVO GRANDE, 1990, 54" x 46", Sandra Townsend Donabed, Wellesley, Massachusetts. In Sandra's beautiful quilt, we see a sense of motion by the contrast of the solid wall and the birds. This is also an excellent example of anticipated motion. Photo by David Caras.

CONTRAST

A feeling of movement can be heightened by contrast. Again, by memory, we realize that some things move and some do not. In CUERVO GRANDE by Sandra Townsend Donabed, the birds seem to have more activity, more potential for movement, because of the contrast with the large wall that appears so immobile (Plate V-4).

Our experience tells us that birds move, but buildings rarely do. The center portion of Sandra's quilt is gold leaf on canvas, inks, and acrylic paints. The outer border is three-dimensional leaves (traced from ivy plants in her yard) attached with rayon braid.

Even nonobjective patterns can display movement through contrast. Because of past experience, we see horizontal lines as quiet and inactive — just as our bodies are resting and still when we are lying horizontally.

Illustration 5-3a. The horizontal lines of this figure are interpreted as quiet and restful.

For a similar reason, we identify diagonal lines as suggesting movement, just as our bodies lean and bend in activities such as sports.

Illustration 5-3b. Notice the natural movement as the player leans forward to hit the ball.

Illustrations courtesy of Corel Draw.

Notice the difference in the figures below. The first figure shows a man ambling along at a slow pace because we see mostly horizontal lines (Illustration 5-4a). However, in the next figure (Illustration 5-4b), we sense more movement, more speed. Why? The figure has more diagonal lines. The arms and legs are all diagonal, not vertical or horizontal. That aspect alone has created more movement.

Illustration 5-4a. The use of mostly horizontal lines suggests little motion of the figure shown.

Illustration 5-4b. More movement and speed is suggested in this figure because of the diagonal lines.

MOTION AS AN ILLUSION

Plate V-5. JOURNEY: LOST/FOUND, 1993, 53" x 53", Emily Richardson, Philadelphia, Pennsylvania. We sense motion in the sweeping color and texture in this beautiful quilt. Photo by Rick Fine.

As seen in CUERVO GRANDE, the horizontal emphasis in the stone wall imparts an inactive feeling. But pure lines without subject reference can give the feeling of motion or may appear unmoving. A quilt such as JOURNEY: LOST/FOUND by Emily Richardson seems dynamic and motion-filled (Plate V-5).

Emily used appliqué with paint embellishment to create this beautiful quilt. It is both constructed and quilted by hand.

Here there are no recognizable objects, no forms that we can identify in fleeting positions. Yet we immediately sense not only the sweeping emphasis, but also the use of spontaneous layering of fabric and textile paint as the quilt artist created this piece.

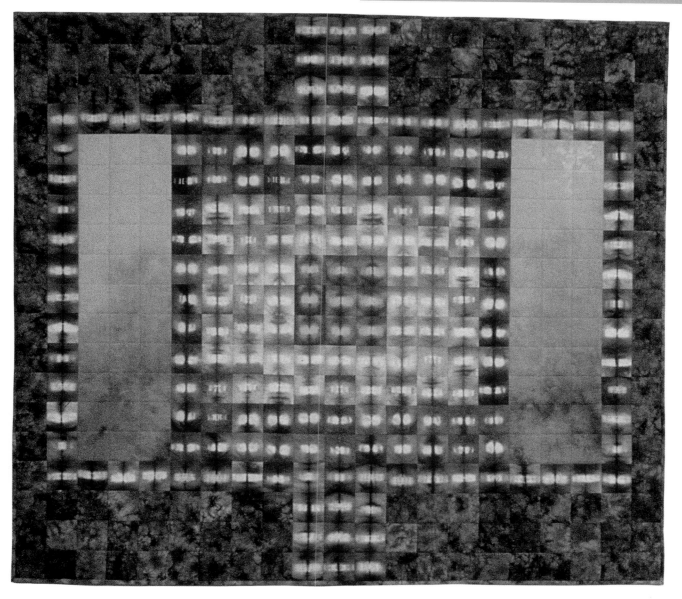

Plate V-6. SEEING IS BELIEVING, 1993, 52" x 47", Jan Myers-Newbury, Pittsburgh, Pennsylvania. Jan's beautiful quilt is tranquil in composition. She machine pieced and quilted this peaceful quilt. Photo by Sam Newbury.

In a similar way, Jan Myers-Newbury's beautiful quilt, SEEING IS BELIEVING (Plate V-6), with its repetition of careful, slowly rendered horizontal and vertical lines seems motionless. Jan uses procion dyes on cotton muslin to hand dye all her fabrics.

Plate V-7. IN THE TEMPLE OF THE GODS, 55" x 39", Jan Myers-Newbury. This quilt shows dynamic motion with its many diagonal lines. A wonderful example of motion and transparency. Photo by Sam Newbury.

By contrast, Jan's quilt IN THE TEMPLE OF THE GODS shows dynamic movement. Notice how the diagonal lines fill this piece with motion. Our eyes are led rapidly over the surface of the quilt and we "see" motion. This is accomplished by the use of diagonal lines.

This quilt is also an excellent example of the illusion of transparency which is explained in detail in Chapter Eight.

VERTICAL HORIZONTAL AND DIAGONAL RELATIONSHIPS

Visual movement in an image often depends on vertical, horizontal, and diagonal relationships. In general, when a shape or line is placed vertically or horizontally in a composition, it will seem stable. Diagonally placed shapes and lines, especially when they are not aligned with an underlying grid, convey movement. Compositions that are full of diagonals tend to look more dynamic than compositions dominated by vertical and horizontal elements. Vertical, horizontal, and diagonal, like dark and light, are forces that can be contrasted and balanced.

The windmill diagram shows equally possible positions for turning blades (Illustration 5-5).

The first image feels frozen. The center windmill is a little more dynamic, but the ends of the blades are aligned on vertical/horizontal axes, again forming a rectangle. The blades of the last windmill give the most convincing appearance of movement because of the asymmetrical diagonal axes.

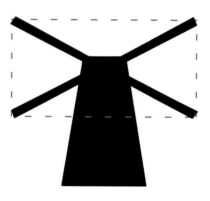

Illustration 5-5. Consider the placement of the windmill's blades to show movement; from frozen rigid to dynamic, asymmetrical diagonal axes.

VERTICAL, HORIZONTAL, AND DIAGONAL QUILT BLOCKS

There are many quilt blocks that show motion by use of vertical, horizontal, and diagonal lines. Some of the following blocks show motion by a distinct diagonal force. The blocks that give the best appearance of motion are the ones that have an asymmetrical diagonal axis, like the windmill.

Tennessee Pine 829.5

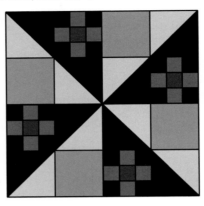

Unnamed 1147

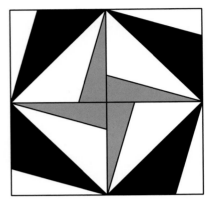

Perpetual Motion 1216

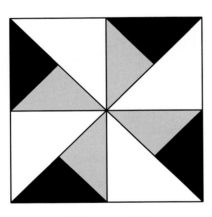

Whirlwind 1266b

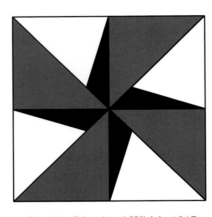

Double Pinwheel Whirls 1267

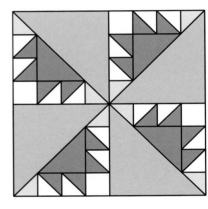

Kansas Troubles 1270

Whirligig 1279

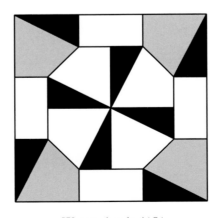

Waterwheels 4151

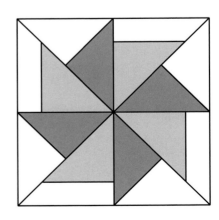

Pinwheel 1294

TRADITIONAL QUILT BLOCKS THAT SHOW MOTION BY THE USE OF VERTICAL, HORIZONTAL, AND DIAGONAL LINES II

Wheel of Fortune 1299

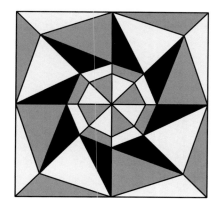

Flying Saucer 1300

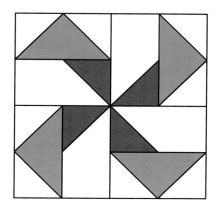

SeeSaw 1336

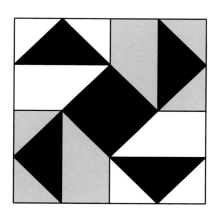

Next Door Neighbor 1337

Spinning L 1406

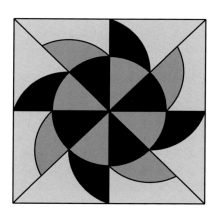

Whirling Dust Storm 1490

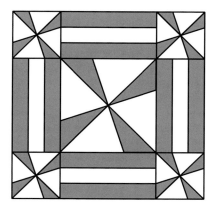

Virginia Reel 2193

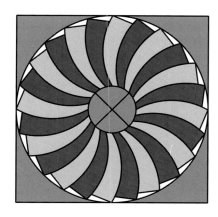

Circular Saw 3544

We are told that talent creates its own opportunities. But it sometimes seems that intense desire creates not only its own opportunities, but its own talent.

Eric Hoffer

MOTION AS AN ILLUSION

TRADITIONAL QUILT BLOCKS THAT SHOW MOTION BY THE USE OF VERTICAL, HORIZONTAL, AND DIAGONAL LINES III

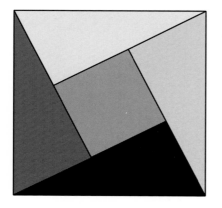

Windmill 2560

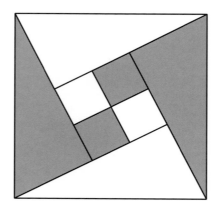

Arabic Lattice 2561

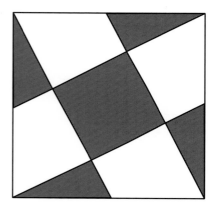

Washington's Puzzle 2562

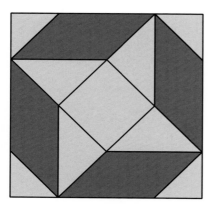

North Star 3950

Unnamed 2564**

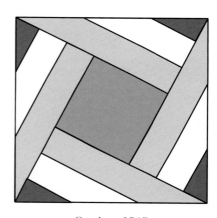

Quebec 2567

Double Windmill 2600

Eccentric Star 2603

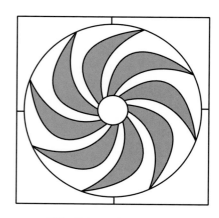

Windblown Daisy 3392

** indicates blocks in pattern section

DIRECTED TENSION

Movement in a still image does not necessarily have anything to do with a photographic likeness of a galloping horse or a bird in flight. A photograph of a form in motion can look absolutely frozen. Movement in a visual pattern is not a consequence of subject matter but comes from the kinds of shapes, angles, curves, and forms that are used. The seeds of motion are already contained in the tensions that are built into every shape and line of a composition.

As long as visual forces are nearly equally distributed, a sense of stillness and balance will prevail. For instance, in a square, the force of the horizontal is about equal to the lift of the vertical.

Because the visual forces are equally distributed, a square illustrates balance and stillness.

An equilateral triangle is almost as still, the thrust of one point is approximately equivalent to the thrust of each of the other two. A stable balance is achieved.

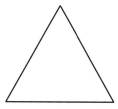

A stable balance is also achieved in an equilateral triangle.

Symmetry creates stillness, especially when its main structural lines are vertical and horizontal. When a symmetrical shape is made asymmetrical, or when the thrust of one direction becomes stronger than that of the others, the sense of energy or tension increases. In Illustration 5-6, the square has become an arena for tensions that pull it strongly in one direction, and the circle, pulled taut along an axis and tipped in one direction, seems poised to roll and to change its shape. Diagonals, along with this kind of distortion, tend to create visual movement.

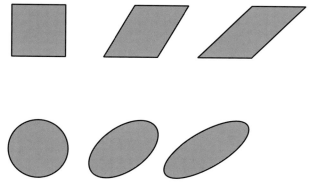

Illustration 5-6.

For the mystic what is how.
For the craftsman how is what.
For the artist what and how are one.

William McElcheran

Plate V-8. THREE FOR THE CROWN, 1987, 53" x 53", Charlotte Warr Andersen, Salt Lake City, Utah. Traditional quilt blocks combined with original pictorial appliqué combine to create an amazing quilt. Notice the backward motion of several horses, created by diagonal lines. Photo from the collection of the Museum of the American Quilter's Society (MAQS).

Motion in a design is directed visual tension. Looking at the quilt THREE FOR THE CROWN by Charlotte Warr Andersen, notice the running horse in the lower right part of the quilt (Plate V-8). We can see how backward-pointing diagonals predominate. In fact, the horse and jockey together form a strong computational triangle that points left and seems drawn to the left-hand edge. In fact it looks as if the horse is running backward. In this amazing quilt, Charlotte combines traditional quilt blocks with original pictorial appliqué.

Plate V-9. BETH'S TRIP TO BALTIMORE, 85" x 100", Beth Gillaspy Allen, Gilbertsville, Pennsylvania. Beth's Baltimore Album quilt displays stillness in its composition and with its beautiful handwork. Photo by AQS.

Compare the orderly stillness in the beautiful quilt, BETH'S TRIP TO BALTIMORE, by Beth Gillaspy Allen (Plate V-9), with the whimsical quilt, ALLEGHENY AVENUE ALBUM by Katherine L. McKearn, Plate V-10.

Plate V-10. ALLEGHENY AVENUE ALBUM, 104" x 104", Katherine L. McKearn, Towson, Maryland. Katherine's quilt conveys movement and unrestrained energy by its use of diagonals and the strong asymmetry of its shapes. Photo by AQS.

In Beth's quilt, the vertical and horizontal gird holds each shape in its grip, and whatever tensions may exist within each shape feel contained and controlled. She used many techniques in contructing this quilt.

Beth hand appliquéd her blocks and used trapunto, embroidery, and inking to embellish her quilt blocks. It is hand quilted.

Katherine McKearn's quilt (shown above), in contrast, seems to undulate and swell. Katherine was inspired by many old Baltimore Album quilts when she made ALLEGHENY AVENUE ALBUM.

She hand and machine pieced, hand appliquéd, embellished, and hand quilted her quilt.

TRADITIONAL QUILT BLOCKS THAT DISPLAY MOTION USING DIRECTED TENSION

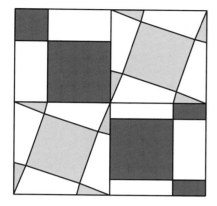

Checkerboard Skew 1048

Mountain Star 1250

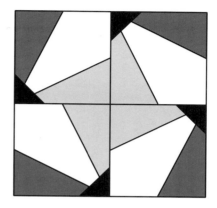

Unnamed 1419

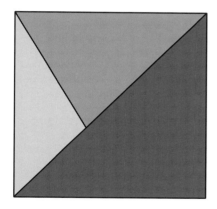

Rocky Mountain 3152

Jacques in the Boat 3192

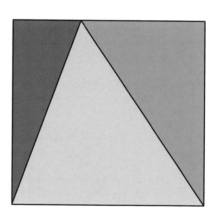

Amber Waves 3288

"If art is to nourish the roots of our culture, society must set the artist free to follow his vision wherever it takes him."
John F. Kennedy

CHAPTER 6

WAYS TO SUGGEST MOTION

Plate VI-1. THE GILGAMESH TAPESTRY, 1984, 96" x 60", Virginia Ferrill Pilard, Berea, Kentucky. Virginia used many techniques to create this extraordinary hanging: batik, reverse dyed fabrics, Seminole piecing, appliqué, embroidery, and embellish. Notice the anticipated motion in the flying birds, the serpent, and the wrestlers. Photo by AQS.

REPEATED FIGURES AND MULTIPLE IMAGES

Over the centuries, artists have devised many practices to present an illusion of motion in art. One of the oldest devices is that of repeating a figure, or using a multiple image. It has been used widely in Oriental cultures as well as in Western medieval art. IN THE GILGAMESH TAPESTRY, by Virginia Ferrill Pilard, we see figures repeated to suggest motion (Plate VI-1).

This hanging was inspired by a study of Sumerian culture, 3000 B.C., the oldest literate culture known to man. The hanging depicts that civilization as revealed in archaeological artifacts. The epic itself was written on twelve clay tablets; Virginia studied at the University of Chicago Oriental Institute to authenticate the data shown in the hanging.

Plate VI-2. SHE COMES IN COLOR, 1988, 72" x 48", Charlotte Warr Andersen. An excellent example of multiple image to suggest motion. Photo by AQS.

This very old technique is still commonly used. The comic strips in our daily newspapers use a series of images in boxes to take our favorite cartoon characters through a sequence of situations that tell a story.

When similar shapes are placed in sequence, we sometimes see movement rather than a random accumulation of shapes. When we see one figure in an overlapping sequence of poses, the slight change in each successive position suggests movement. This is what happens from one frame to the next on a filmstrip, and the term "stroboscopic motion" comes from the stroboscope, a primitive moving picture machine. It happens in still images as well. In SHE COMES IN COLOR by Charlotte Warr Andersen, the overlapping of the silhouettes increases the sense of a single motion (Plate VI-2).

Charlotte machine pieced the ribbons and hand appliquéd the figures in this lovely quilt. It was quilted by hand.

TRADITIONAL QUILT BLOCKS THAT USE MULTIPLE IMAGES TO ILLUSTRATE MOTION

Pine Tree Quilt 854

Unnamed 1026

Cradle Quilt 1066

Double Star 1304.3

The Square Deal 1966

Flying Geese 1967

Priscilla's Dream 2082

Odd Fellows Chain 2170**
** indicates blocks in pattern section

Milady's Fan 3340

When the number of shapes increases and a gradient is added, the sense of movement becomes even stronger. In Illustration 1-5 (page 20), the graduating triangles are part of a continuous and smooth movement, and by their repetition, the dynamic effect is strengthened.

STRAIGHT
CURVES

This is another of my favorite illusions, showing curves using only straight lines. It could also be called curves without curves. This illusion is magically created when diagonal lines change from 45° to many other angles. The angled lines gener-ate curves on the surface, although only straight-line piecing is involved (Illustrations 6-3 and 6-4).

In addition, when multiple-size rectangles and squares are used in the same design, the surface seems to bend or create other undulating patterns such as we see in Illustration 6-5.

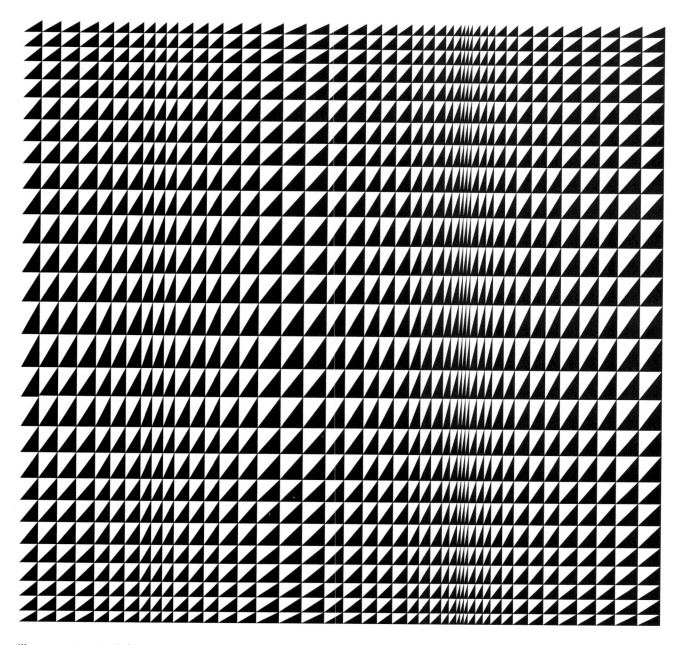

Illustration 6-3. Angled lines generate curves over the surface of this design.

Illustration 6-4.

Illustration 6-5. When multiple-size rectangles and squares are used in the same design, the surface seems to bend.

Plate VI-3. IRISH EYES, 1991, 72" x 84", Irma Gail Hatcher, Conway, Arkansas. Irma combined several traditional patterns, Irish Chain and a Pineapple Star variation, to create a dynamic illusion of straight curves. Photo by AQS.

    Straight curves can create some dramatic movement over the surface of a drawing or quilt as we see in IRISH EYES by Irma Gail Hatcher (Plate VI-3). We see multiple curves where only straight piecing is present.

    Irma combined the traditional patterns Irish Chain and a Pineapple Star variation to create this example of straight curves.

Optical Illusions for Quilters

TRADITIONAL QUILT BLOCKS THAT USE THE ILLUSION OF STRAIGHT CURVES

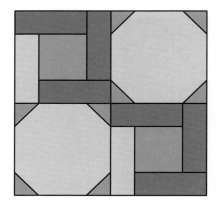

Around the Twist 1028.5

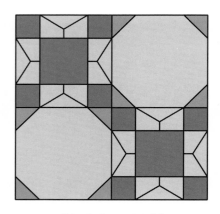

Block Star 1029**

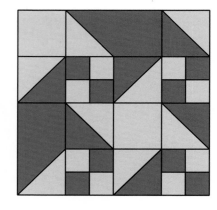

Indiana Puzzle 1142a

The Eight Pointed Star 1624

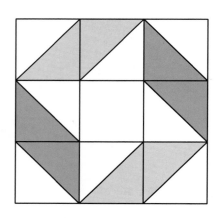

Ribbon Quilt 1657

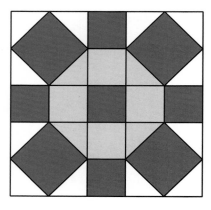

Rolling Square 1932

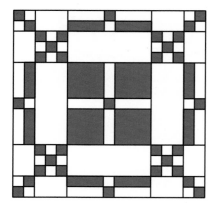

Burgoyne's Quilt 2098d

Irish Chain 2114

** indicates blocks in pattern section

TRADITIONAL QUILT BLOCKS THAT CREATE THE ILLUSION OF STRAIGHT CURVES BEST WHEN SET SIDE BY SIDE

Storm at Sea 2187

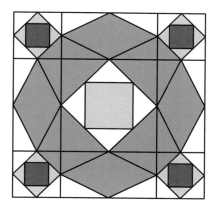

Rolling Stone 2188b

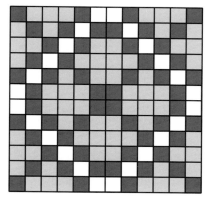

Double Irish Chain 2284a

Virginia Reel 2397**

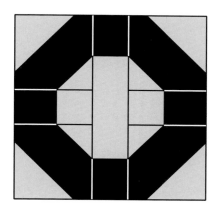

Wedding Ring 3235

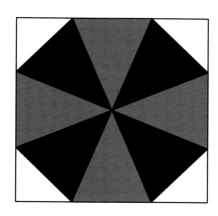

Kaleidoscope 2704

Pineapple 2635

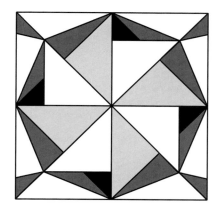

Lucky Star 1301

Road to Fortune 1299

** indicates blocks in pattern section

Optical Illusions for Quilters

QUILT BLOCKS THAT USE THE ILLUSION OF STRAIGHT CURVES BEST
WHEN SET SIDE BY SIDE WITH ALTERNATING BLOCKS

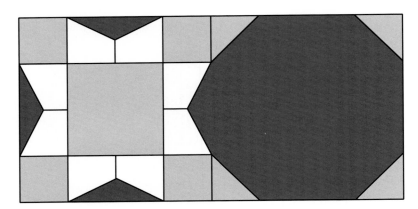

Block Star 1029

Block Star set side by side. Full-size patterns are provided in the pattern section on pages
154-156.

FUZZY OUTLINE

We interpret a photograph as a symbol of movement. With a fast shutter speed, moving images are frozen into stop-action photographs. Look at the photo of the author riding the tea cup ride at Walt Disney World (Plate VI-4). Here the shutter speed is relatively slow, so the background becomes a blurred, indistinct image that we read as movement. This is an everyday visual experience. When objects move through our field of vision quickly, we do not get a clear mental picture of them. A car may pass us on the highway so fast that we perceive only a colored blur. Details and edges of the form are lost in the rapidity of the movement.

MOVEMENT AND CHANGE

A gradient is a gradual change in a visual element. It might be a change in direction, like the "S" curve of a swan's neck (Illustration 6-4), or a change in tone or value, like the gradual movement from light to dark. A gradient changes slowly and evenly, leading the eye smoothly and in equal steps without sudden jumps from one point to the next.

Plate VI-4. The author riding the tea cup ride in Disney World, 1988. Notice the blurred background suggesting rapid movement.

Illustration 6-4. The "S" curve in the swan's neck is a gradual change and illustrates a change in direction.

Illustration courtesy of Corel Draw.

Plate VI-5. AUSTRALIS, 1988. 81" x 73", Fiona Gavens, New South Wales, Australia. A wonderful example of blurred edges to suggest motion. Photo by Fiona Gavens.

The blurred outline in the quilt AUSTRALIS by Fiona Gavens clearly suggests flowing movement (Plate VI-5). Fiona machine pieced and machine quilted her work. The blurred edges of the quilt suggest the movement of water and are an excellent example of motion using a blurred outline.

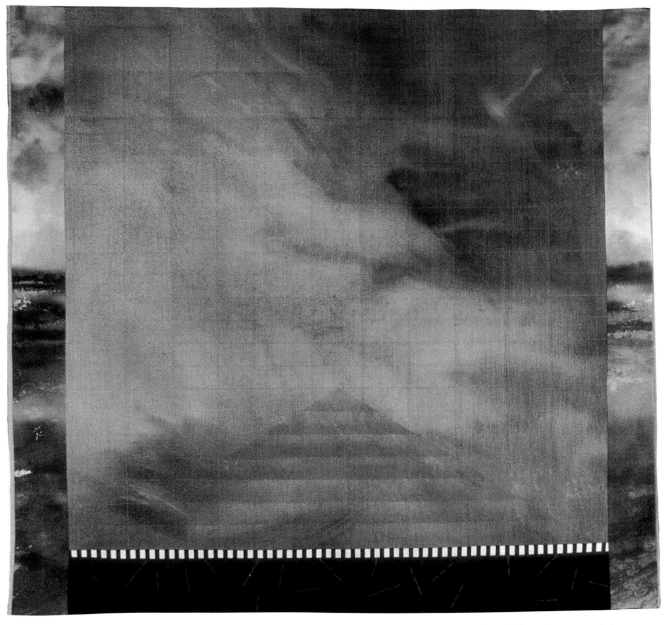

Plate VI-6. NIGHTWATCH, 1988, 40" x 40", Elizabeth A. Busch, Glenburn, Maine. Use of airbrushed acrylic paint and dye painting create great spatial depth and sweeping movement in this graceful and beautiful quilt. Photo by Elizabeth A. Busch.

Even in purely nonobjective art quilts, the blurred edge serves as an effective device. The sweeping shapes in NIGHTWATCH by Elizabeth A. Busch clearly suggest flowing movement as your eyes move across the surface of the quilt (Plate VI-6).

Elizabeth used many techniques to create this beautiful quilt. She airbrushed the surface with acrylic paint and also dyed painted the surface. It is machine pieced, hand embroidered, and hand quilted.

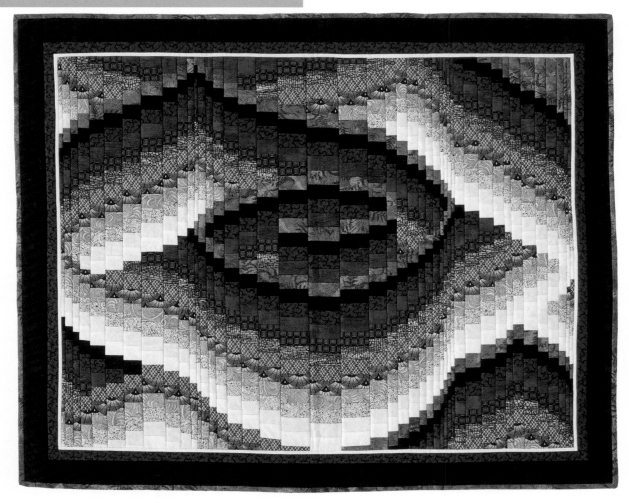

Plate VI-7. HURRICANE GEORG, 1993, 40" x 33", Georgia Schmidt, Lake Jackson, Texas. Gradients in color and size create a marvelous example of movement in this quilt using advanced bargello techniques. Photos from <u>Bargello Quilts</u> by Marge Edie, reprinted with permission from That Patchwork Place, publisher. Photographer Brent Kane.

(To purchase a copy of <u>Bargello Quilts</u>, visit your local quilt shop or call That Patchwork Place at 1-800-426-3126).

Gradients create visual motion. In the quilt HURRICANE GEORG by Georgia Schmidt, the gentle swelling, tapering, and curving shapes generate a series of lively movement and countermovement (Plate VI-7).

Georgia designed this lovely and lively quilt in an advanced bargello class.

More than one kind of gradient can be applied to the same form or used in the same composition, and each can enhance the sense of motion. If a taper, and then a gradient of curve and direction, and finally a change from light-to-dark are added to the simple shape, each addition causes the scene to appear more animated.

Plate VI-8. FANTASIA, 93" x 95", Donna Radner, Chevy Chase, Maryland. An original design using strip piecing. Donna machine pieced this quilt that demonstrates vigorous movement. Quilting was done by Fannie Horst. Photo by AQS.

Another example of using gradients is Donna Radner's quilt FANTASIA (Plate VI-8). Donna designed her quilt by strip piecing subtle color gradations. Cut into different widths, she developed the intertwining bargello design in this marvelous quilt. We also see an illusion of depth using overlap.

Notice how the eye moves in the direction of diminishing intervals. The tendency is also to see movement from larger, heavier forms to smaller, lighter ones, just as when we look from the near brightness or darkness to the pale or light distance in the quilt.

Plate VI-9. MISSION ACCOMPLISHED, 1992, 50" x 43", Edith Zimmer, San Diego, California. This was Edith's first attempt at making a pictorial quilt. She spent about four weeks working on this quilt, which is a wonderful example of depth, overlap, and movement using changes and contrast. Photo by AQS.

Notice how the dark wall in MISSION ACCOMPLISHED by Edith Zimmer looms dark and large in the foreground, and how our eyes move to the distant tower, which is lighter and smaller (Plate VI-9). Edith was inspired by the photography of Ansel Adams. She began by sketching her quilt on a piece of white fabric pinned to a flannel wall. She used a blue washout pen so she could easily change her lines as needed. When the drawing was complete, she traced it onto paper, which she then cut apart and used as templates.

As she finished appliquéing each section of her design, she pinned it to its proper place on her fabric drawing, which remained pinned to the wall throughout the entire process. This way, she could be assured that her work in progress was producing the desired results.

Plate VI-10. VERMONT SWIMMERS, 1992, 77" x 82", Catherine McConnell, Pittsburgh, Pennsylvania. A superb example of time displayed in a quilt. Catherine transfers her photos to fabric and machine pieces and quilts her pieces. Photo by Catherine McConnell.

TIME

Seeing occurs in time as well as space. When we watch a ball roll across the floor, it moves through a period of a few seconds as well as moving from one side of the room to the other.

In a drawing of the same subject, however, the work is entirely still. The illusion of three dimensions can be presented in two-dimensional art, but how is the fourth dimension, *time*, dealt with in a medium in which there is no time? In the real world, one moment is followed by another. How can this motion be translated into a form in which nothing moves?

Plate VI-11. CLOUD SWIMMERS, 1993, 36" x 24", Catherine McConnell. Again, we see moments of time captured in this splendid quilt. Photo by Catherine McConnell.

In one method, the artist can use the classic comic strip format to subdivide an event into close-paced moments. Here each separate box marks a small step forward in time, almost as in a stroboscope. We see different, progressive aspects not only of an extended movement, but of a single complex action.

Early in this century, cubist painting gave us the image of many moments in time, many glances, many viewpoints, brought together in a single painting. This method is used in two quilts by Catherine McConnell.

In VERMONT SWIMMERS (Plate VI-10) and CLOUD SWIMMERS (Plate VI-11), we see snapshots capturing the moment. We see many bits of time, many viewpoints of the swimmer brought together to form a single quilt. Catherine used a photo transfer to imprint her photographs on fabric. She then machine pieced and quilted her work.

The assemblage of snapshots captures something of the way things are always seen in time. The image is built up from several little glimpses. The collective details and bits of information register in the eye and mind of the viewer who has the time to sit and look for more than a few moments.

"Art washes away from the soul the dust of everyday life."
Picasso

CHAPTER 7

COLOR MAKING SPACE

Color can be an important tool in our quilts. We can use it with perspective or the other illusionary tools to intensify the sense of depth. However, color can also create space by itself.

There is a direct relationship between color and a visual impression of depth or pictorial space. Let's explore this.

COLOR TEMPERATURE

It may seem strange to identify a sensation of temperature with color which is entirely visual. However, experiments have been done to prove the phenomenon.

One experiment, as described in the book, *The Art of Color* (Itten), found a difference of five to seven degrees in subjective feeling of heat or cold between a workroom painted blue-green and one painted red-orange. In the blue-green room the occupants felt that 59° was cold, but in the red-orange room occupants did not feel cold until the temperature fell to 52°-54°. The first color scheme seemed to slow down the circulation and the second one seemed to stimulate it.

Generally yellow, yellow-orange, orange, red-orange, red, and red-violet are referred to as warm, and yellow-green, green, blue-green, blue, blue-violet, and violet as cool or cold (Illustration. 7-1).

In general, cool colors tend to recede from the surface, while warmer hues tend to come forward. This is

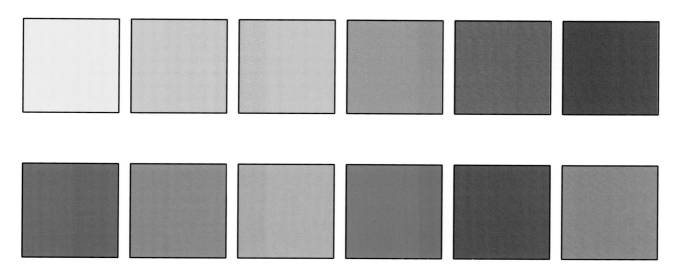

Illustration 7-1. Warm colors: yellow, yellow-orange, orange, orange-red, red, and red-violet.
Cool colors: violet, blue-violet, blue, blue-green, green, yellow-green.

caused by slight muscular reactions in our eyes as we focus on different colors. It is also a visual memory. In reality, when distant objects are viewed, they seem cooler in color because of the intervening depth of air; they also take on a bluish color. Cool-warm contrast contains elements that suggest nearness and distance.

However, this cold-warm classification can be misleading. Blue-green is always cool and red-orange is always warm, but the hues between them on the color wheel may be either warm or cool according to the warmer and cooler tones with which they are contrasted.

We can use this rule and bend it if we are skillful and imaginative. Like all rules dealing with color, it can be bent and shaped to create wonderful effects.

For instance, place a small square of an electric blue fabric on a larger square of dull brownish red (Illustration 7-2). Make sure the intensities are the same, that they are both the same value and brightness. The electric blue should recede and the red should come forward. However, in this case it does not. Why? A pure color advances relative to a duller one of equal brilliance. Since the red was dull, the pure blue advanced.

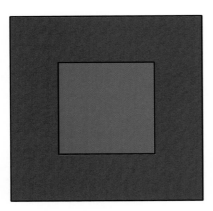

Illustration 7-2. A pure color will always advance relative to a duller color.

Some warm colors recede into the background when they are surrounded by even warmer colors. Putting a slightly blue-red next to an orange-red (Illustration 7-3) causes the blue-red to recede even though it is a warm color.

Illustration 7-3. Warm colors recede into the background when they are surrounded by even warmer colors.

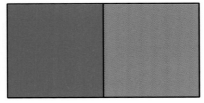

As we have seen, colors are adaptable and ever-changing depending on their surroundings. If you want warm colors to appear even warmer, put them next to cool colors. Notice how the orange almost glows next to the blue-green (Illustration. 7-4).

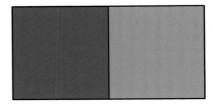

Illustration 7-4. If you want warm colors to appear even warmer, put them next to cool colors. The warm orange almost glows next to the cool blue-green.

The opposite also applies. If you want to accentuate cool colors, put them next to warm colors. A blue-green will appear cooler when viewed next to a clear yellow (Illustration 7-5).

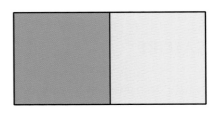

Illustration 7-5. Cool colors will be accentuated by placing them next to warm colors. The cool blue-green is highlighted when placed next to a clear yellow shade.

We can also bend these rules to make warm and cool colors react differently. If you want a cool color to advance, place it next to a colder cool color (Illustration 7-6). When the same blue-green is placed next to another cool color, blue-violet, it will appear warmer. Even though both colors are cool, the blue-green advances because the blue-violet is cooler.

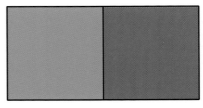

Illustration 7-6. Cool blue-green will advance when placed near an even cooler color, blue-violet.

Plate VII-1. Trees encased in ice after a storm of freezing rain, showing the colors of ice; white, blue, and blue-violet. Photo by Karen Combs.

Black is usually considered a warm color, perhaps because black absorbs heat. White is usually considered a cool or colder color because it reflects heat; white is also identified with ice and snow. To make almost any color appear cooler, add the colors of snow and ice: white, blue, and blue-violet, to the color (Illustration 7-7 and Plate VII-1).

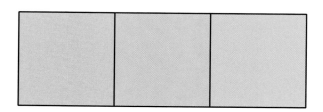

Illustration 7-7. The colors of snow: white, blue, and blue-violet, make any color appear cooler.

Black and white also can help colors advance or recede. Any light tone on a black background will advance according to its degree of brilliance (Illustration 7-8).

This effect is also seen on a white background. Shades approaching black are thrust forward when placed on white (Illustration 7-9).

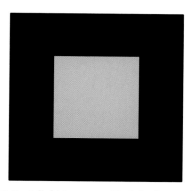

Illustration 7-8. A light tone on a black background advances.

Illustration 7-9. The dark color is thrust forward when placed on white.

When equally brilliant blue-green and red-orange are seen against black, the blue-green retreats and the red-orange advances. Refer to the examples below to better visualize how this principle works (Illustration 7-10a, b, c, d).

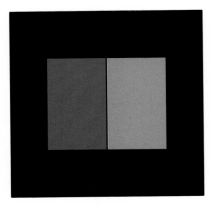

Illustration 7-10a. When equally brilliant blue-green and red-orange are placed against black, the blue-green retreats and the red-orange advances.

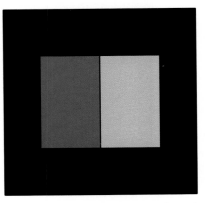

Illustration 7-10b. When the red-orange is lightened, it advances even more.

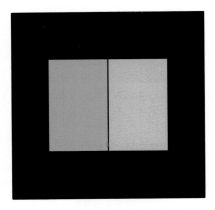

Illustration 7-10c. If the blue-green is lightened, it advances to the same level as the red-orange.

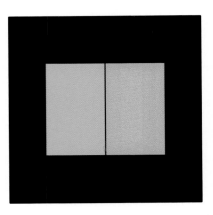

Illustration 7-10d. When the blue-green is lightened even further, it advances and the red-orange recedes.

Plate VII-2. MRS. TAFT'S CHOICE, 1996, 32" x 40", Karen Combs. Notice how the cool blue-green background recedes and the warm red-orange advances in this example of color creating depth in a quilt. Photo by Charles R. Lynch, American Quilter's Society.

In MRS. TAFT'S CHOICE by Karen Combs, the use of both warm and cool colors creates depth over the surface of the quilt (Plate VII-2). As you look at it, the warm red-orange advances while the cool blue-green recedes.

You can also use color's spatial effects to create either an illusion of depth or a flat, one-dimensional pattern.

If you want to accentuate the illusion of flatness in your quilt, try using hues of the same color temperature. This tends to void the advance of one color over the other. To further the flatness, minimize all contrasts as much as possible and keep all the values the same (Illustration 7-11).

Illustration 7-11. The illusion of flatness is achieved when all contrast is eliminated and the values are kept the same.

COMPLEMENTARY CONTRAST

Complementary colors are opposite each other on the color wheel. There is a color complementary to every given color. Some examples of complementary pairs are

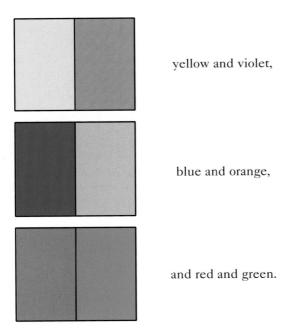

yellow and violet,

blue and orange,

and red and green.

Illustration 7-12. Complementary colors are opposite each other on the color wheel.

Neighboring hues on the color wheel induce their complement or opposite in each other. For example, if yellow and orange are adjacent, the yellow will appear slightly greener than if it were by itself, and the red will appear cooler and a little more purple (Illustration 7-13).

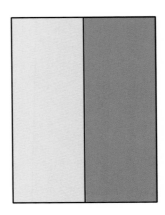

Illustration 7-13. Neighboring colors on the color wheel produce their complement or opposite in each other.

The tendency of a strong color is to induce its opposite in a neutral color. For instance, a spot of gray on an orange background will appear bluish (Illustration 7-14). The induced hue is strongest when the neutral and the color are the same value.

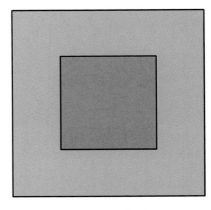

Illustration 7-14. A strong color will induce its opposite in a neutral color.

Optical Illusions for Quilters

COLOR AND VALUE

Color values are important in spatial illusions. Whether working with color or with values of black and white, pay strict attention to value control to obtain the greatest illusion of depth.

Whatever colors are used, high contrast comes forward visually, and areas of lesser contrast generally recede.

As we saw in Illustration 7-11, if all the values are the same, the surface will look flat. Also, if the same texture, value, and color are used, the surface appears flat.

Contrasts intensify each other. A straight line will accentuate the curve of an arc. We use this principle in our quilting designs. An intricate patchwork design is enhanced by a plain quilting design and a plain patchwork design is strengthened with a fancy quilting design (Illustration 7-15).

 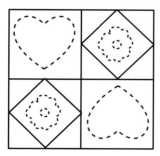

Illustration 7-15. The quilting design can enhance the patchwork pattern.

The contrast of color can also create illusions. Blue emphasizes the warmth of orange (Illustration 7-16). This contrast sometimes causes a sense of vibration.

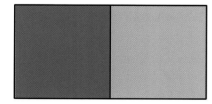

Illustration 7-16. Contrast can cause illusions. The cool color, blue, emphasizes the warm color, orange.

Accordingly, an intense vermilion on a strong blue-green background also appears to glow and pulsate (Illustration 7-17).

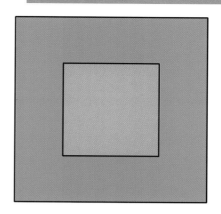

Illustration 7-17. Strong contrasts like vermilion on blue-green may cause colors to glow and pulsate.

Black against white produces a strong contrast and makes gray and white seem brighter (Illustration 7-18).

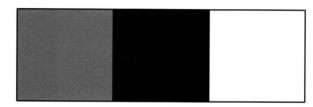

Illustration 7-18a. Black makes white seem brighter.

Illustration 7-18b. White and black triangles combine to make a bold statement.

A light hue, such as light green, will appear weak and whitish when placed on a black background. The strong contrast in value overpowers the lighter color. Black against white produces a strong contrast and the white seems brighter (Illustration 7-19).

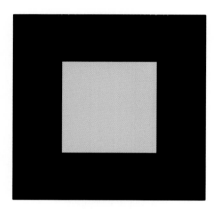

Illustration 7-19. Light green is overpowered by a black background and appears weak and whitish.

The same color will seem more vivid when placed on a white background (Illustration 7-20).

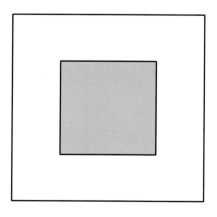

Illustration 7-20. The same light green is more vivid when placed on a white background.

For the same reason, a spot of dark blue or red on white (Illustration 7-21) will look almost black and colorless, whereas on black these pigments will appear more brilliant (Illustration 7-22).

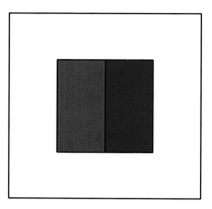

Illustration 7-21. When dark blue or red is placed on a white background, it appears black and colorless.

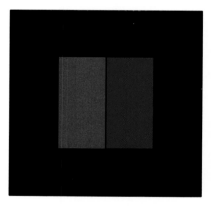

Illustration 7-22. When the same colors are placed on black, they appear to be more brilliant.

This tendency of a strong value contrast to overpower and neutralize color and brightness can be used to advantage. For example, light contrasting colors that are vivid can be harmonized by surrounding or outlining them in black. Repetition of the black also helps unify the design. Stained glass windows, in which each pane is outlined with black lead, demonstrate this principle.

Plate VII-3. VICTORIAN TULIPS, 1983, 81" x 87", Glenys R. Nappo, Oak Ridge, Tennessee. Black unifies the solid colors in this beautiful example of a stained glass window quilt. Photo by AQS.

In VICTORIAN TULIPS by Glenys R. Nappo, we see black unifying the solid fabrics and creating a pleasing design (Plate VII-3). Glenys was inspired to create this quilt by her love of stained glass windows. She developed the design using a combination of two patterns from a book of stained glass pattern designs.

The same harmonizing effect is produced by outlining or surrounding dark, vivid colors with white, silver, or gold.

LIGHT, ATMOSPHERE, LANDSCAPES, AND SEASCAPES

There are some observations we can make as we look at the use of color in pictorial quilts. These observations also help enhance the illusions of depth or space.

Color is not only looked at, but also looked into. Volume color refers to the way color by itself can create atmosphere and space.

Think of a large fish tank filled with blue-tinted water. The nearest fish are easy to see, perhaps bright, yellow tropical fish. Those yellow fish deeper in the tank look greenish because of the blue water, and at the back of the tank, they almost disappear, blending into the blue distance.

LIGHT

Light acts as an agent that softens and gently dissolves forms in the depths of the picture plane. The close objects are sharp and clear, but as we look into the depth of the picture plane, the objects become softer.

Plate VII-4. Light softens the features of the distant hills and lake. Photo by Karen Combs.

ATMOSPHERE

Because of the intervening depth of air, the color of more distant objects always seems cooler.

Plate VII-5. Distant hills appear bluer than the hills in the foreground. Photo by Karen Combs.

Although it has nothing to do with parallel lines or vanishing points, this kind of space, gently and evenly receding into the distance, is often called atmospheric perspective. This simply means that objects — landscape forms, trees, buildings, and mountains — take on the color of the light and lose their own color as they get farther and farther away. They are absorbed into the colorful atmosphere (Plate VII-6).

Plate VII-6. Distant hills are absorbed into the colorful atmosphere. Photo by Karen Combs.

This occurs because the dust in the earth's atmosphere breaks up the color rays from distant objects and makes them appear bluish. As the objects recede, any brilliance of color becomes more neutral, finally seeming to be gray-blue.

LANDSCAPES AND SEASCAPES

As we just discussed, in landscapes more distant objects always seem cooler in color because of the intervening depth of air.

In an seascape, we generally picture the water as blue or blue-green. However, the closer the water is to us, the more yellow green the water will be. The farther away the water is, the bluer it appears.

Knowing these rules of color in nature will help you create a quilt that has a realistic look.

Plate VII-7. Notice the distant hills are more neutral in color than the hills and trees in the foreground. Photo by Karen Combs.

Plate VII-9. Incoming waves at the Gulf of Mexico, Florida, appear very yellow-green. Photo by Karen Combs.

Plate VII-8. Broken clouds accentuate the colors of the sky. Photo by Karen Combs.

Plate VII-10. The deeper the water, the bluer it appears. Photo by Karen Combs.

OPTICAL ILLUSIONS USING COLOR

"Every child is an artist. The problem is how to remain an artist once he grows up."   Pablo Picasso

IRRADIATION

Having looked at various rules and observations about color and value, let's look at several illusions using color.

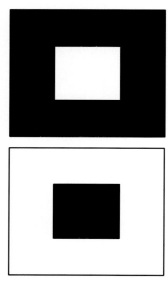

Illustration 8-1. A white square on a black background appears larger than a black square on a white background.

Irradiation is an optical illusion that causes a white area (or an intense color) seen against a dark background to appear larger than it is really. The area seems to radiate light, appearing as a glowing blur that expands beyond its edges. Thus, a white square on a black ground seems larger than a black square of the same size on a white ground (Illustration 8-1).

This effect is sometimes called halation. It creates an opposite result, so that an intense light background will overlap the boundaries of a dark shape seen against it and make the dark shape appear smaller.

BRIGHTNESS AND CONTRAST

The eye discriminates differences between shades of gray in terms of relative brightness. A given area is judged light or dark as it is compared with an adjacent area of darker or lighter values. Areas equal in value will be consistently judged unequal if they are viewed against contrasting reference backgrounds. The gray circle below appears darker against the white background and lighter against the black background. We see the same illusion with the gray squares (Illustrations 8-2a and 8-2b).

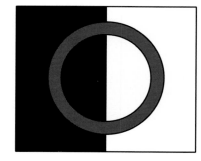

Illustration 8-2a. The gray circle appears darker against a white background and lighter against a black blackground.

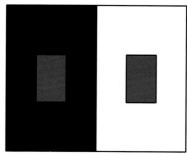

Illustration 8-2b. Notice the same illusion with the gray squares.

AFTER-IMAGE

Another peculiar visual phenomenon is called after-image. After looking at bright objects, we see after-images of the same size and form which vary more or less in color. These "visual left-overs" are due to persistence or fatigue of the visual process, depending upon conditions. After looking at the sun for a moment, the very bright sensation of the sun's presence is seen.

After-images may be produced by looking intently at any object and then directing the eyes toward a blank surface, such as a wall. A picture frame will be seen as a rectangular after-image; a checkered pattern will be seen as a checkered after-image. After-images are best observed when the eyes are well rested.

Stare at an area of intense color for a minute or so, and then glance away at a white piece of paper or wall. Suddenly, an area of the complementary color will seem to appear. For example, when you look at the white wall after staring at an orange shape, a definite blue area in somewhat the same shape will seem to take form on the wall (Illustration 8-3).

Try this with the orange square below.

Illustration 8-3. To produce an after-image, stare at this orange square for 60 seconds, then glance away at a white wall or piece of paper.

To find the after-image of fabric, cut out a small square and place it on a piece of white paper. Stare at it for a minute or so and then look away at a white wall or another white piece of paper to see the after-image.

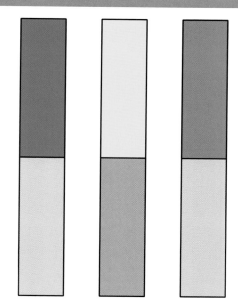

Illustration 8-4. Each color has its own after-image; it will be that color's complementary color.

Every color has its own after-image. It will be that color's complementary color or the color directly across from it on the color wheel (Illustration 8-4). The after-image will be somewhat lighter in value than the original color, e.g., the after-image of sky blue is peach, the after-image of clear yellow is a lavender, and so on.

After-images play many subtle parts in painting and can also be used in our quilts. For example, in a painting where a gray-blue sky meets the horizon of a blue-green body of water, the involuntary eye movements may produce a pinkish line just above the horizon. This is the after-image of the blue-green water creeping upward by eye movements.

You can use after-image as an accent color in your work. Look for small areas in a design that would be a good placement for the after-image of your primary color. It can fortify the appearance of your dominant color and add to the beauty of your quilt.

NEGATIVE AFTER-IMAGES

Retinal fatigue is one factor for the phenomenon of negative after-images. As the viewer gazes steadily at high contrast black and white figures, small gray spots begin to appear on the intersections of the crosses below (Illustration 8-5).

This illusion works best when high contrast black and white figures are used. You can see this demonstrated in the illustration where a less intense contrast is present between the white and gray areas (Illustration 8-6).

Staring intently first at a white cross on a black background and then at a blank white wall or piece of paper will result in a black negative after-image.

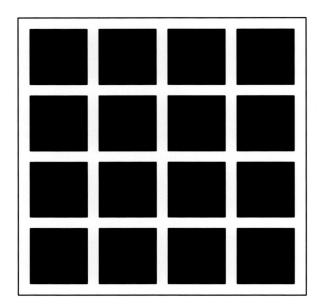

Illustration 8-5. Retinal fatigue causes small gray spots to appear ar the intersections of the white lines.

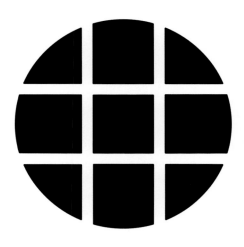

Illustration 8-7. Stare at this design and then at a white wall to create a negative (black) after-image.

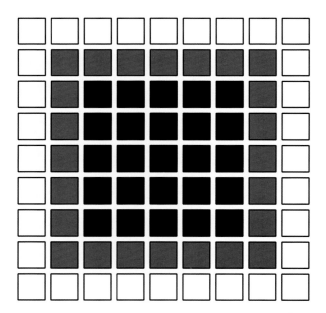

Illustration 8-6. Notice this illusion works best in the high contrast black and white areas of this design.

Plate VIII-1. SKYLAR'S QUILT, 1995, 33" x 43", Deanna Smith Apfel, Philo, California. Deanna designed this quilt for her godson, Skylar. It's an excellent example of transparency. Photo by Deanna Smith Apfel.

TRANSPARENCY

Transparency is a subtle and beautiful illusion. It is the illusion of layers, of something transparent being laid over or under something else.

In SKYLAR'S QUILT by Deanna Smith Apfel, we see the illusion of white squares being laid over the darker background (Plate VIII-1).

Plate VIII-2. ELLIOTT'S STAR GARDEN, 1995, 42" x 42", Sally Nadelman, New Berlin, New York. Sally designed this beautiful transparency quilt after taking a class on transparency. Machine pieced and hand quilted. Photo by Sally Nadelman.

Another example of transparency is ELLIOTT'S STAR GARDEN by Sally Nadelman (Plate VIII-2). In this quilt, we see the illusion of a layer of white showing through multi-colored stars.

With transparency, we can "see" through the first layer to the second. We achieve this by manipulating the color and lines within our quilt blocks.

Plate VIII-3. ILLUSION #2, 89" x 88", Caryl Bryer Fallert, Oswego, Illinois. The original design for this quilt was drawn using Corel Draw and is one in a series of quilts where Caryl is exploring the illusion of overlapping transparent triangles. Photo by AQS.

In ILLUSION #2 by Caryl Bryer Fallert, we see a fantasic example of the illusion of transparency using overlapping triangles (Plate VIII-3). Caryl pieced the triangles from strips of fabric, hand dyed in value (light to dark) gradations of three primary colors (turquoise, yellow, fuchsia), and three secondary colors (green, orange, purple). Each triangle was pieced separately and then cut into horizontal strips. The strips of two triangles were alternated when they were sewn back together. This creates the illusion of more than one triangle occupying the same space. As the groups of triangles were sewn together, the illusion of long vertical diamonds appeared in the background.

The illusion of transparency can be created by several methods:

Method 1. Pick any two colors. The transparency will occur where they overlap. Use the darker value of one of the colors in this spot.

It may help to think of the colors as a family; you have the father (blue) and the mother (green). Their child, the transparency, is a blue slightly darker than the father.

Use colors that are the same intensity. Colors can be all vibrant, grayed, or light, but they need to be the same intensity.

Method 2. Use analogous colors. Analogous colors are simply colors that are next to each other on the color wheel. An example of analogous colors is blue, blue-violet, violet or red, red-orange, orange

Use the two outside colors in your block, and in the overlapping section, use the middle color.

Again, if we think of the colors as a family, we have the father (yellow-orange), the mother (red-orange) and the child is the middle color (orange).

In the overlapping color (child color), use the same value or a slightly darker value than the parents.

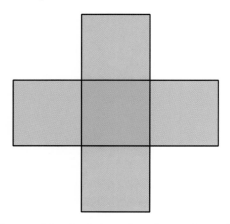

Illustration 8-9. Use the darker value of one color in the center of the cross to produce a transparency.

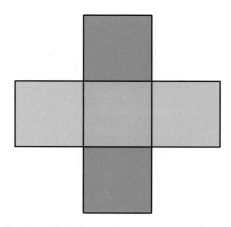

Illustration 8-10. Pick three colors next to each other on the color wheel. Use the middle color in the center of the cross to produce a transparency.

Method 1. Darker value, where blue and green overlap; a darker blue is created.

Method 2. Analogous colors; where yellow-orange and red orange overlap, an orange is created.

Method 3. The blending method is fun! Do you remember mixing paints when you were in school? We can do the same thing with this method of transparency.

Think about the three primary colors: blue, yellow, and red. When you mix blue and yellow, you get green; when you mix red and blue, you get purple; or you can mix yellow and red to make orange.

Use this knowledge to create a transparent look. In this transparency, the parents are the primary colors and the child is the created color. Where the pieces overlap, use the created color.

As we have already discussed, warm colors advance (red, orange, yellow) and cool colors recede (blue, green, purple). You can use this movement to your advantage in transparency. The warm color will frequently look as if it is on top.

Method 4. The last method is the illusion that a sheer color or fabric has been laid over a brighter color. To create this illusion, select a lighter, paler or grayed version of one of the colors where they overlap.

Again, we have the father (rust), the mother (cream), and the child, the middle color (light rust).

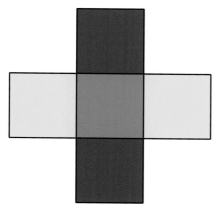

Illustration 8-11. Mix two colors to produce a third color. Use the third color in the center of the cross to produce a transparency.

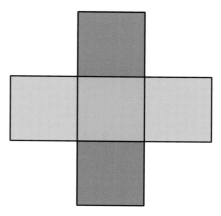

Illustration 8-12. Use a lighter value of one color in the center of the cross to produce a transparency.

Method 3. Blending colors, where blue and yellow overlap, a green is created.

Method 4. Lighter value, where rust and cream overlap, a light rust is created.

OPTICAL ILLUSIONS USING COLOR

COLORING WORKSHEET

Examples of all four methods, darker values, analogous colors, blending colors, and lighter values, have been presented. Try each method by coloring the squares below. Copy this page for your own use and try your own variations.

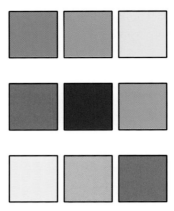

Illustration 8-13. Blending colors produces a third color. Blue and yellow makes green. Red and blue makes purple. Yellow and red make orange.

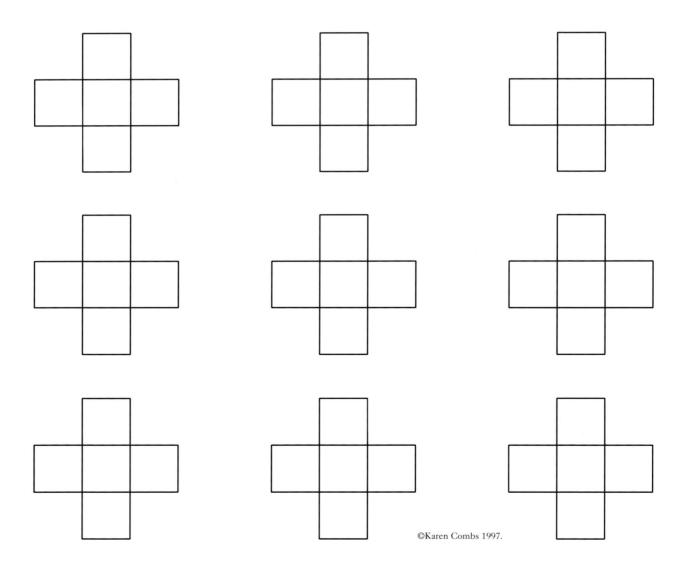

©Karen Combs 1997.

TRANSPARENCY QUILT BLOCKS

Now that we know the colors to use, where do we put them? In the quilt block Kentucky Chain there is an overlapping area. This is where the transparency can occur or where the created or child color should be used. Each method of transparency is demonstrated.

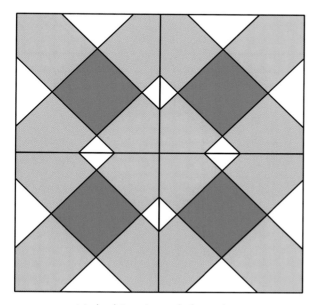

Method 1, using a darker value.

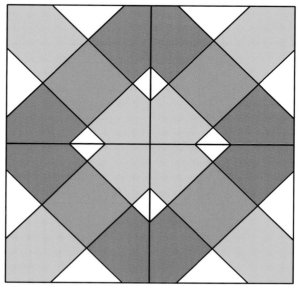

Method 2, using analogous colors.

Method 3, using blended colors.

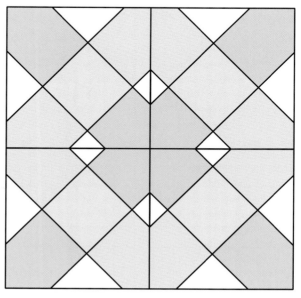

Method 4, using a lighter value.

Many traditional quilt blocks lend themselves to transparency. Examine the blocks in the illustration below and look for an overlapping area. Use the child color in that area.

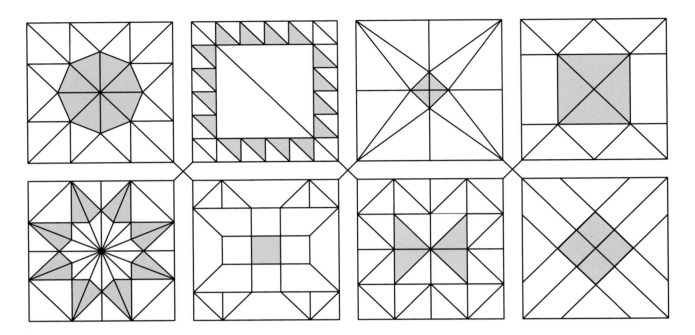

You can create your own original transparent quilt blocks. Look at any traditional quilt block and notice where you can add a line to create an overlapping area. Use the examples below to stimulate your imagination.

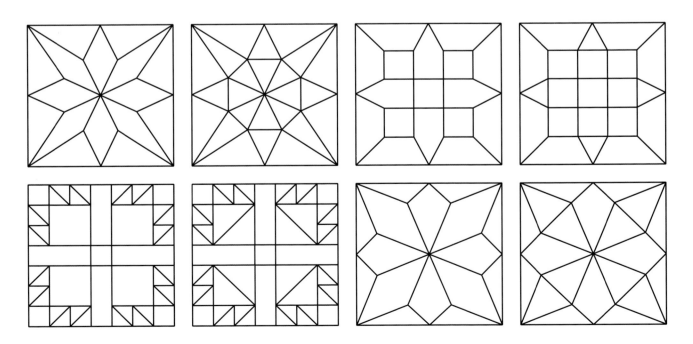

TRADITIONAL QUILT BLOCKS THAT HAVE AN OVERLAPPING AREA, PERFECT FOR A TRANSPARENCY

Gothic Pattern 1167

Four Corner Puzzle 1212

Tangled Star 1244

Carpenter's Square 2580

Interlocked Squares 2618

Love's Chain 4094

Double Link 4189**
(Friendship Links)

The Four Corners 4191
** indicates blocks in pattern section

Double Square 4192

Some of the visual puzzle quilt blocks are wonderful to use with the illusion of transparency. Look for areas that overlap. If no overlapping areas exist, look for areas where you can add a line or two to create an overlapping area.

BLOCK & QUILT PATTERNS

CUPS AND SAUCERS

Beginner Level

This easy block shows the illusion of depth and also the illusion of motion.

Color placement

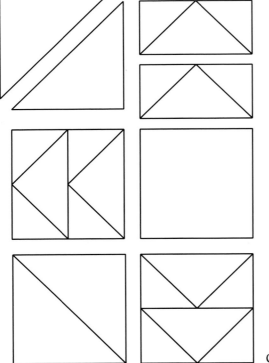

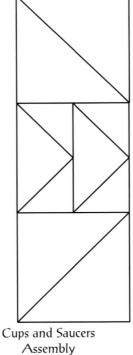

Cups and Saucers
Assembly

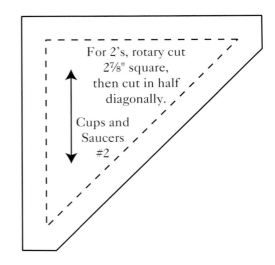

For 2's, rotary cut
2⅞" square,
then cut in half
diagonally.

Cups and
Saucers
#2

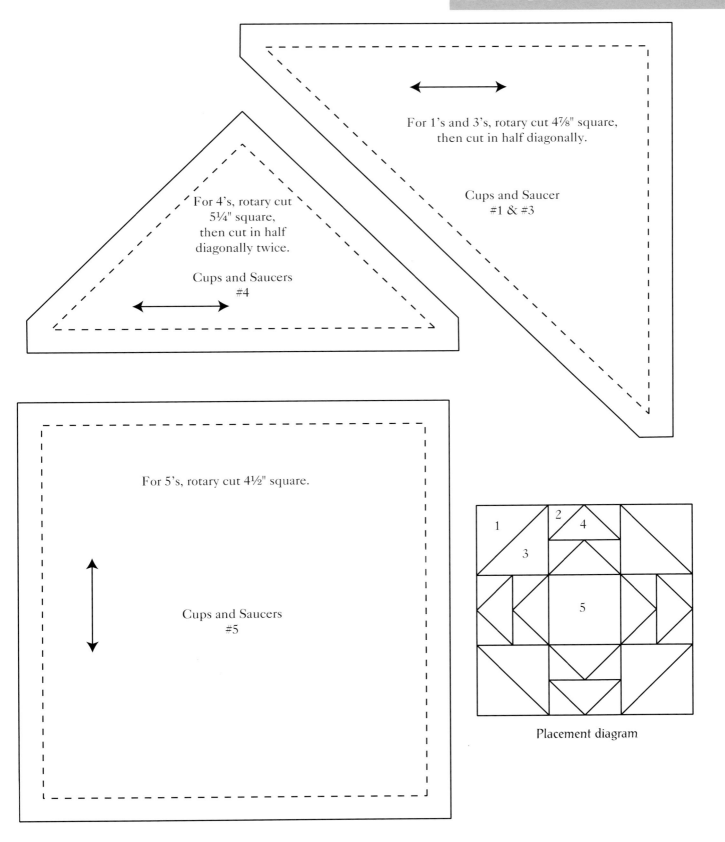

For 1's and 3's, rotary cut 4⅞" square, then cut in half diagonally.

Cups and Saucer
#1 & #3

For 4's, rotary cut
5¼" square,
then cut in half
diagonally twice.

Cups and Saucers
#4

For 5's, rotary cut 4½" square.

Cups and Saucers
#5

Placement diagram

SQUARES AND OBLONGS

Intermediate Level

This simple block has a good illusion of depth. I used hand-dyed fabric in an eight-step gradation to increase the look of depth. Place the deepest color in the center of the block to maximize the illusion.

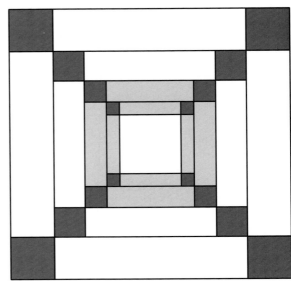

Color placement

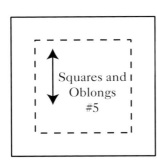

Squares and Oblongs
#1

For 1's, rotary cut
2⅜" square.

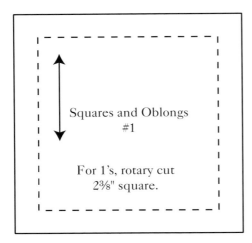

Squares and
Oblongs
#5

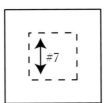

#7

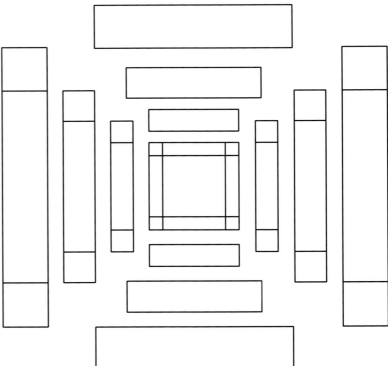

Squares and Oblongs Assembly

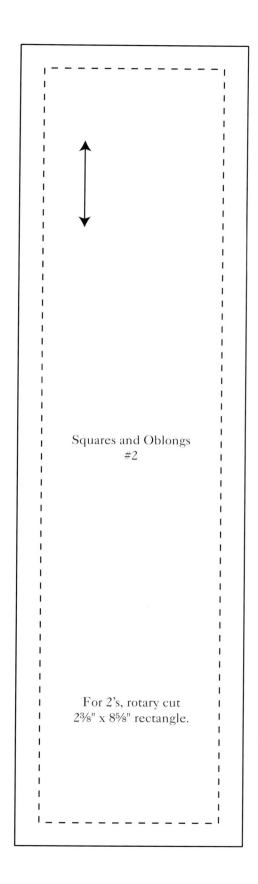

Squares and Oblongs
#2

For 2's, rotary cut
2⅜" x 8⅝" rectangle.

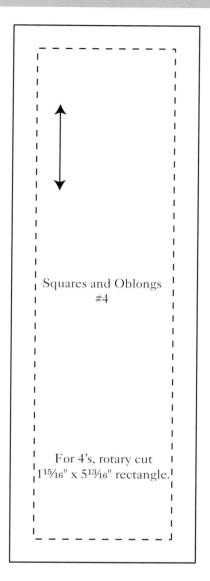

Squares and Oblongs
#4

For 4's, rotary cut
1¹⁵⁄₁₆" x 5¹³⁄₁₆" rectangle.

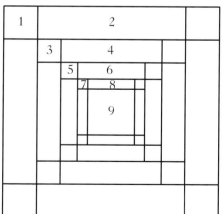

Placement diagram

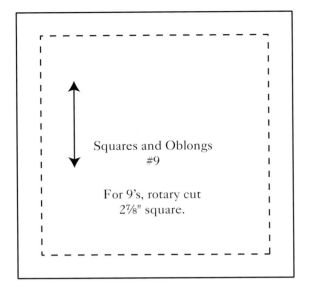

Squares and Oblongs
#9

For 9's, rotary cut
2⅞" square.

For 5's, rotary cut 1½" square.

For 6's, rotary cut 1½" x 3⅞" rectangle.

For 7's, rotary cut 1" square.

For 8's, rotary cut 1" x 2⅞" rectangle.

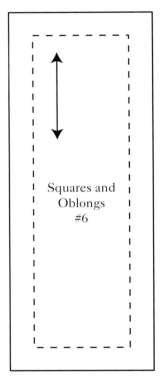

Squares and
Oblongs
#6

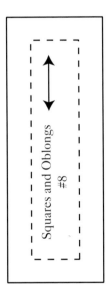

Squares and Oblongs
#8

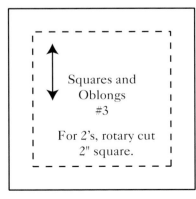

Squares and
Oblongs
#3

For 2's, rotary cut
2" square.

FRIENDSHIP LINKS (DOUBLE LINKS)

Beginner Level

An interesting block that looks more complicated than it is. This block is perfect for the illusion of transparency.

Color placement

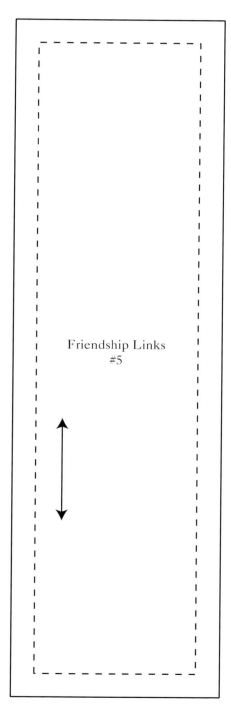

Friendship Links
#5

For 5's, rotary cut 2³⁄₁₆" x 7¼" rectangle.

Friendship Links Assembly

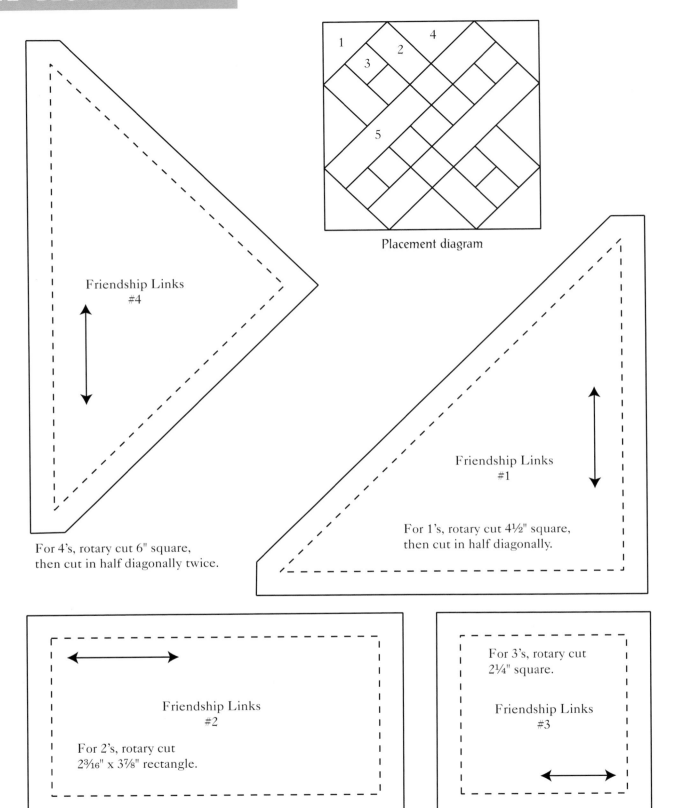

Placement diagram

Friendship Links
#4

For 4's, rotary cut 6" square,
then cut in half diagonally twice.

Friendship Links
#1

For 1's, rotary cut 4½" square,
then cut in half diagonally.

Friendship Links
#2

For 2's, rotary cut
2³⁄₁₆" x 3⅞" rectangle.

For 3's, rotary cut
2¼" square.

Friendship Links
#3

UNNAMED

Beginner Level

This skewed star has a subtle but effective illusion of motion. Use fabric with lots of color and texture for a contemporary look.

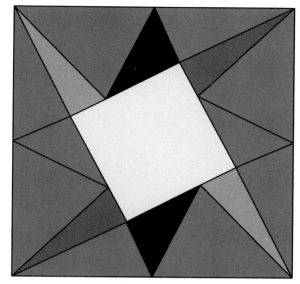

Color placement

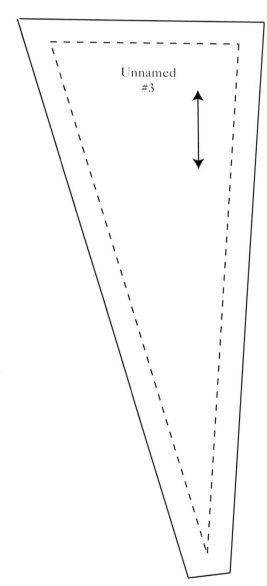

Unnamed #3

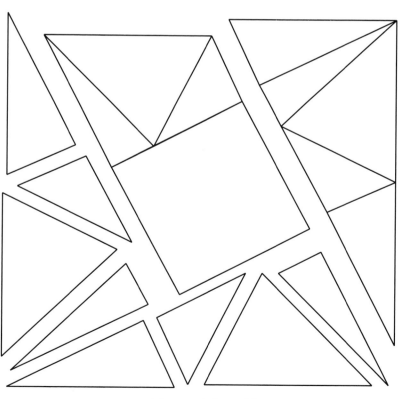

Unnamed Assembly

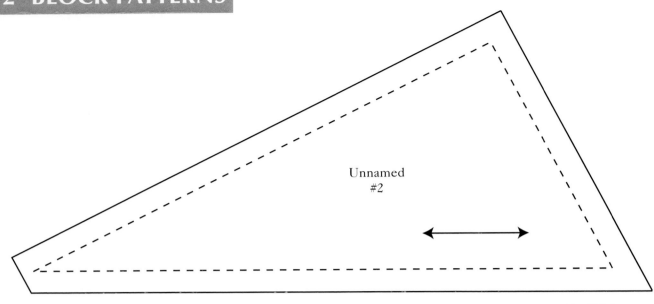

Unnamed
#2

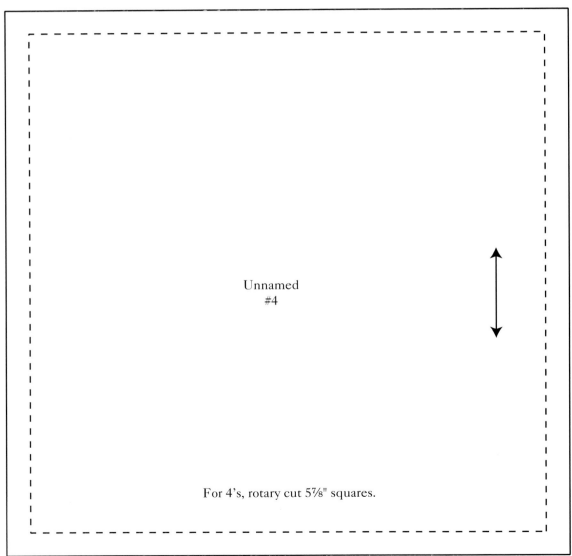

Unnamed
#4

For 4's, rotary cut 5⅞" squares.

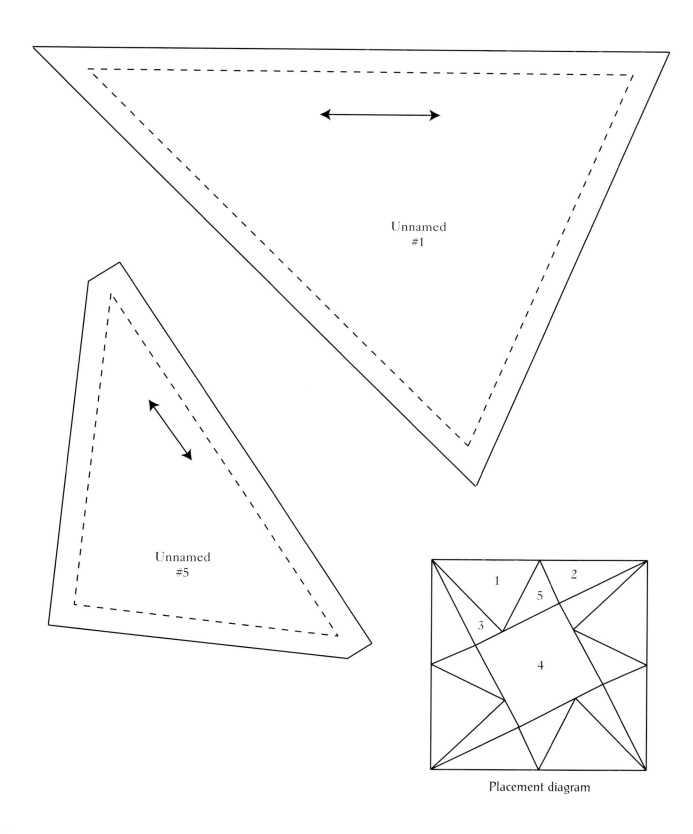

Unnamed
#1

Unnamed
#5

Placement diagram

ODD FELLOWS CHAIN

Beginner Level

Multiple pieces make this block a bit harder to piece, but is well worth the work. This block has the illusion of depth and the illusion of motion. A blue to orange hand-dyed gradation enhances the illusion of depth.

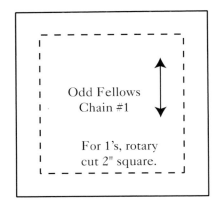

Odd Fellows Chain #1

For 1's, rotary cut 2" square.

Color placement

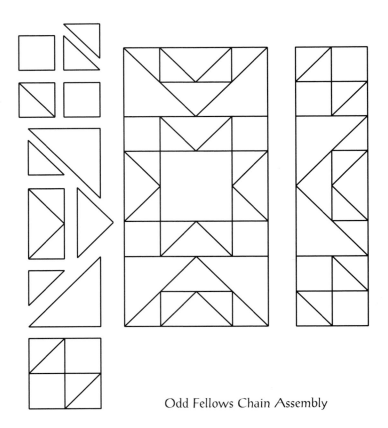

Odd Fellows Chain Assembly

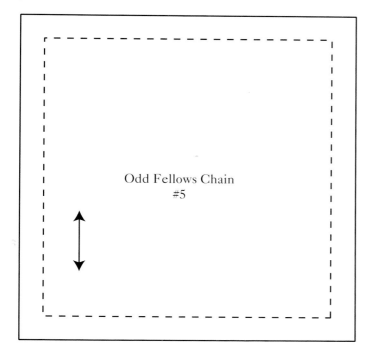

Odd Fellows Chain
#5

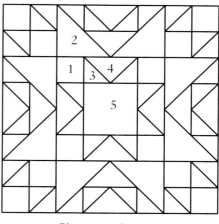

Placement diagram

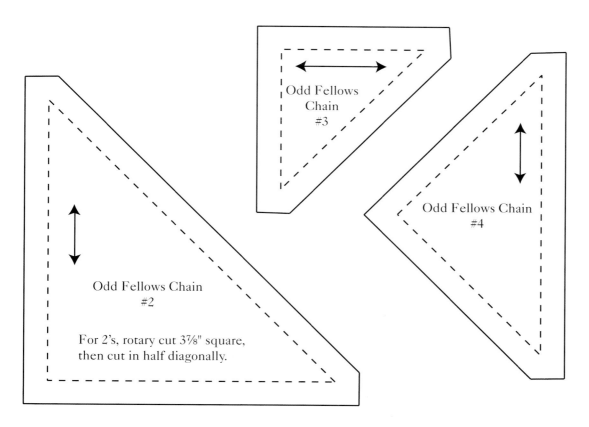

Odd Fellows
Chain
#3

Odd Fellows Chain
#4

Odd Fellows Chain
#2

For 2's, rotary cut 3⅞" square,
then cut in half diagonally.

VIRGINIA REEL

Beginner Level

This is one of my favorite illusion of curves. Simple to piece, but very beautiful when the blocks are set side by side.

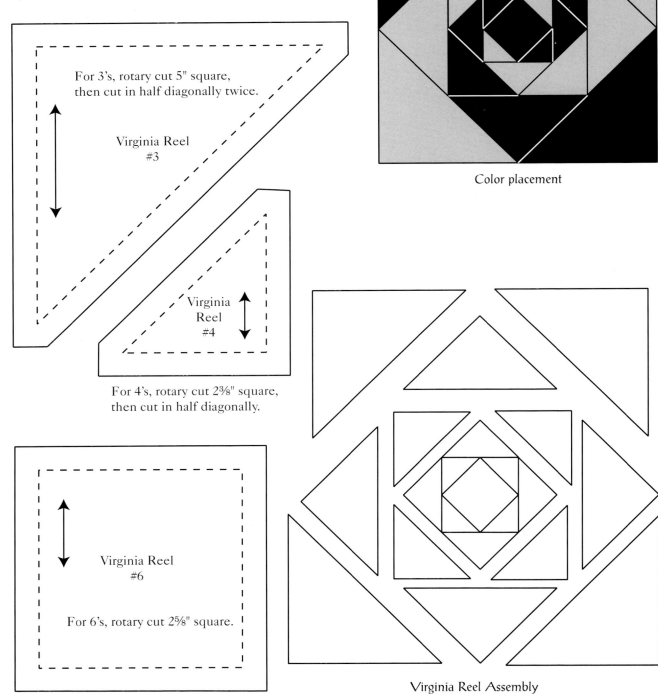

Color placement

For 3's, rotary cut 5" square, then cut in half diagonally twice.

Virginia Reel
#3

Virginia
Reel
#4

For 4's, rotary cut 2⅜" square, then cut in half diagonally.

Virginia Reel
#6

For 6's, rotary cut 2⅝" square.

Virginia Reel Assembly

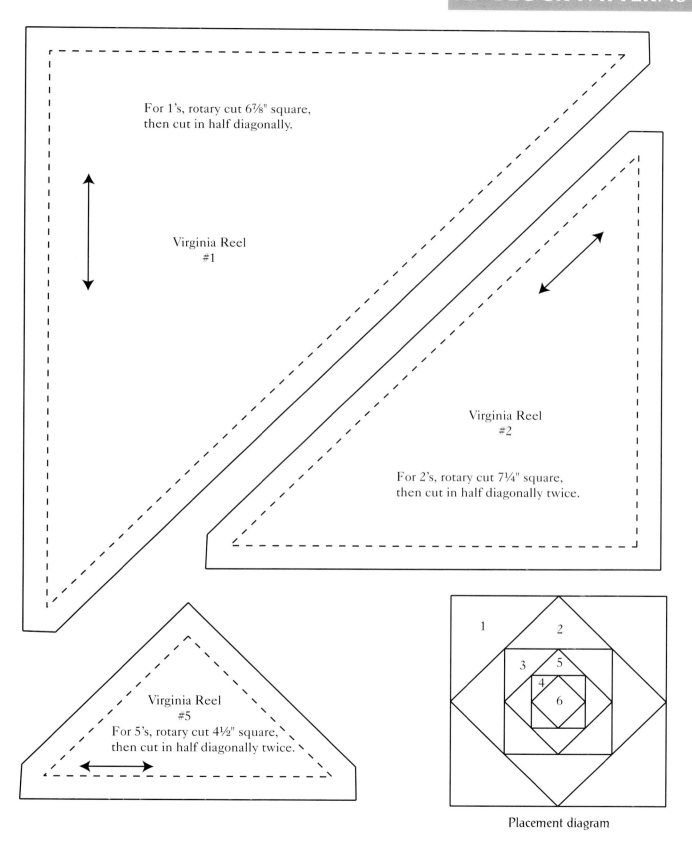

For 1's, rotary cut 6⅞" square,
then cut in half diagonally.

Virginia Reel
#1

Virginia Reel
#2

For 2's, rotary cut 7¼" square,
then cut in half diagonally twice.

Virginia Reel
#5
For 5's, rotary cut 4½" square,
then cut in half diagonally twice.

Placement diagram

TRANSPARENT PINWHEEL

Beginner Level

Easy to piece, lovely when used with the illusion of transparency.

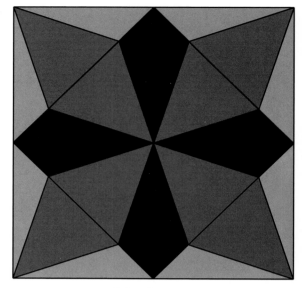

Color placement

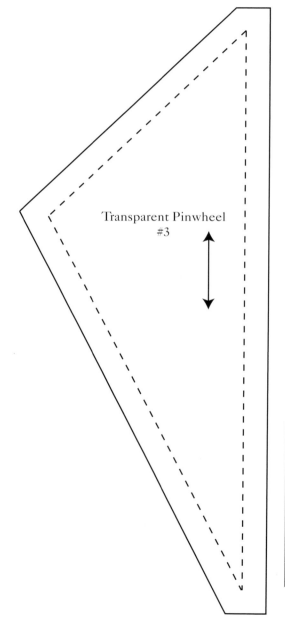

Transparent Pinwheel
#3

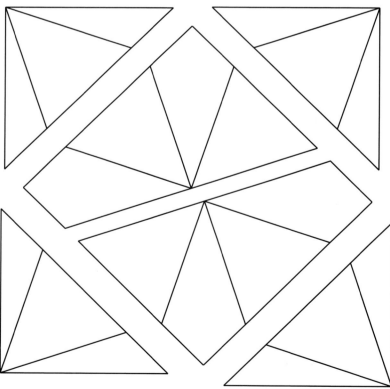

Transparent Pinwheel Assembly

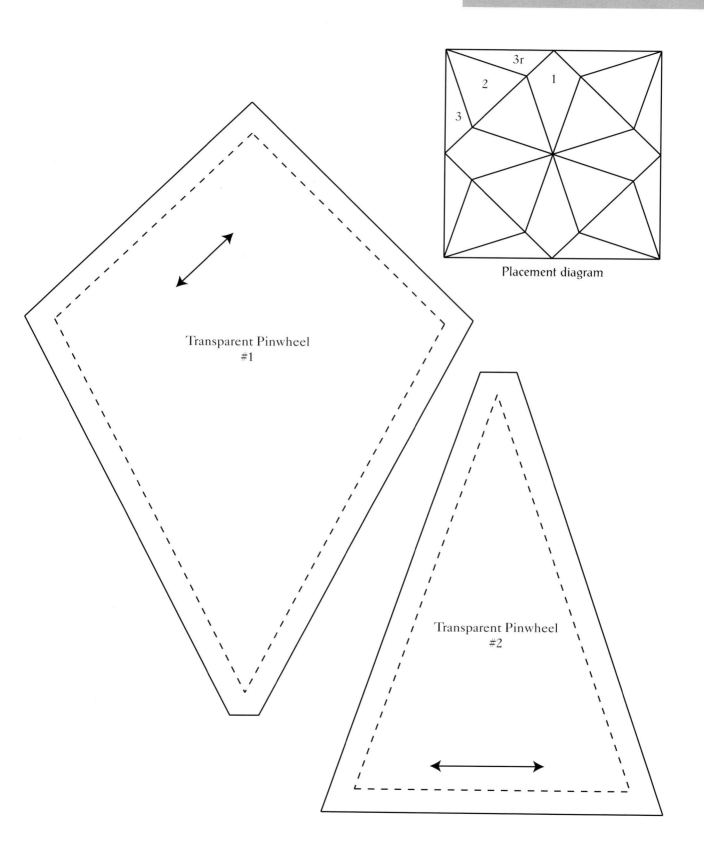

Placement diagram

Transparent Pinwheel
#1

Transparent Pinwheel
#2

BLOCK STAR

Intermediate Level

A block with a few set-in corners, but well worth the effort. A beautiful illusion of "straight" curves.

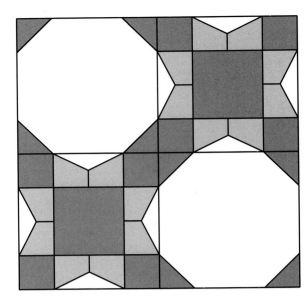

Color placement

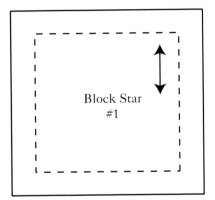

For 1's, rotary cut 2" squares.

For 2's, rotary cut 2⅜" squares, then cut in half diagonally.

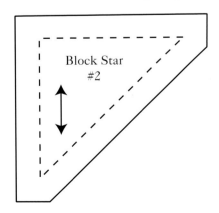

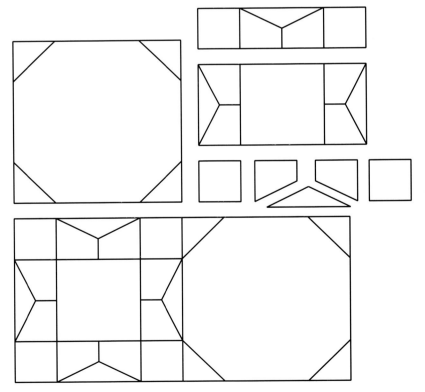

Block Star Assembly

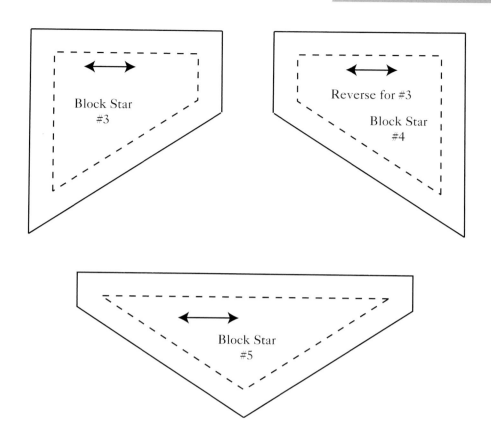

Block Star
#3

Reverse for #3

Block Star
#4

Block Star
#5

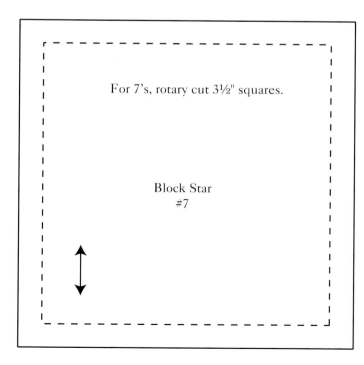

For 7's, rotary cut 3½" squares.

Block Star
#7

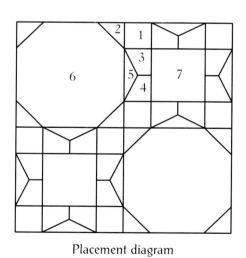

Placement diagram

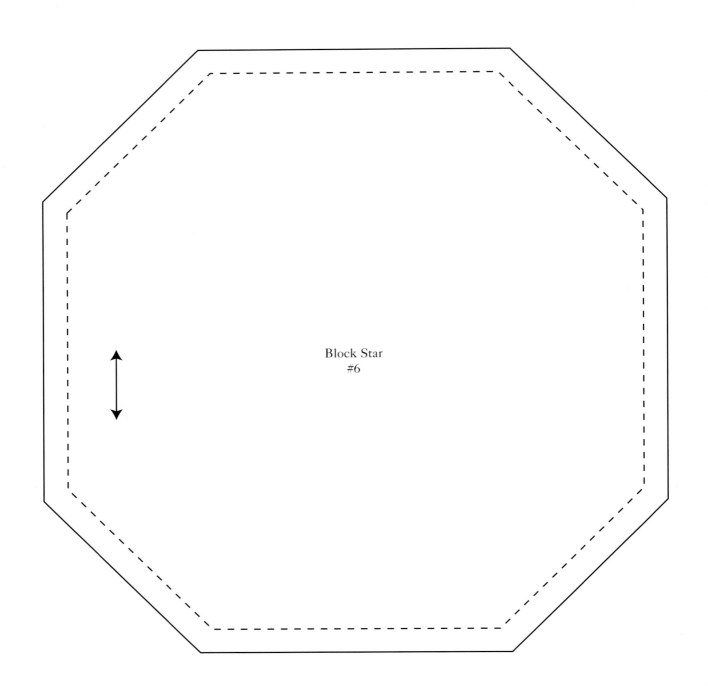

Block Star
#6

QUILT PROJECT

HARLEQUIN CUBE
28" x 31"

This quilt is a striking design with the illusion of depth. It is featured on the cover of this book. Designed, pieced, and hand quilted with Sulky® Sliver™ and Prizm Hologram thread by Karen Combs.

FABRICS

Various dark, medium, and light scraps in cool colors: blue, green, and purple

Various dark, medium, and light scraps in warm colors: red, yellow, and orange

Optional: Lamé may be cut and added for sparkle

BACKGROUND

½ yd. black fabric, cut for 30" x 33" appliqué

BINDING

½ yd. black fabric, cut (4) strips 2" x 44"

CUTTING

(12) Template #1's, *assorted values

(96) Template #2's, *assorted values

(12) Template #3's, *assorted values

*See pattern pieces on page 159 for correct breakdown.

ASSEMBLY

1. Construction is based on a 3-D Churn Dash block. First, piece the basic shapes together. These pieces can be pieced by hand or machine. Use a ¼" seam allowance. Press carefully. Since most of the pieces have a bias outside edge, handle them with care. Piece the rows together and remember to offset by ¼" when joining to create points.

2. Piece center first. Sew the patchwork in rows, paying close attention to the color placement.

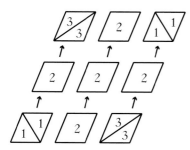

Sew diamonds into rows.

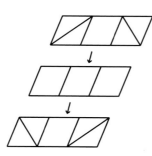

Sew rows together.

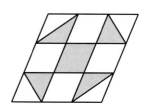

Sew dark and medium sides together, stopping ¼" from the end.

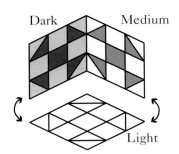

Set in light colored block.

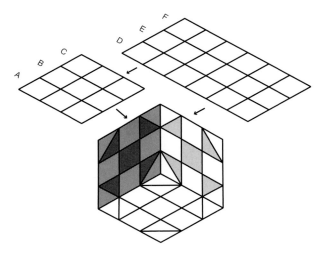

Assembly diagram

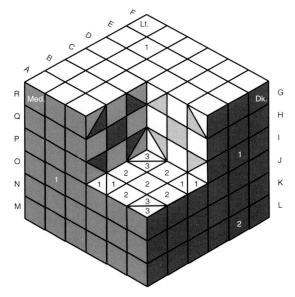

Harlequin Cube placement diagram.

3. With right sides together and matching points, stitch the dark block to the medium block. Stop ¼" from the end to permit the blocks to pivot.

Set in the light colored block to form a cube.

4. Piece according to the placement diagram shown. The use of a flannel design wall that has been tacked up, will be extremely helpful in keeping track of all the pieces as you sew and press.

Starting with light side, row A, sew diamonds together to form a row. Sew all rows on light side the same way, press and replace on flannel.

Join together sewn rows A, B, and C, remembering to offset. Press and sew onto dark side of block.

Sew together long rows D, E, and F, remembering to offset. Press and sew onto row C and cube of blocks.

Place medium colored diamonds to make rows M – R. Press and place on flannel.

Sew together rows P, Q, and R. Press and add set into remaining side of block. Sew together rows O, N, and M. Press and set into remaining side. Press lightly being careful not to stretch the cube.

Place dark diamonds to make rows G – L. Press and place on flannel. Sew together short rows G, H, and I. Press and set into medium side of block and light top. Sew together long rows J, K, and L. Press and add onto bottom of block.

5. Center cube onto background fabric and appliqué into place.

6. Design Options — The background may be cut larger if desired and borders may be added. Press thoroughly being very careful not to stitch it out of shape. Trim background to square up design if desired.

7. Quilting — Layer quilt top with batting and backing of your choice and finish with hand or machine quilting.

8. Binding — Cut four strips 2" x 44". Bind as desired by hand or machine.

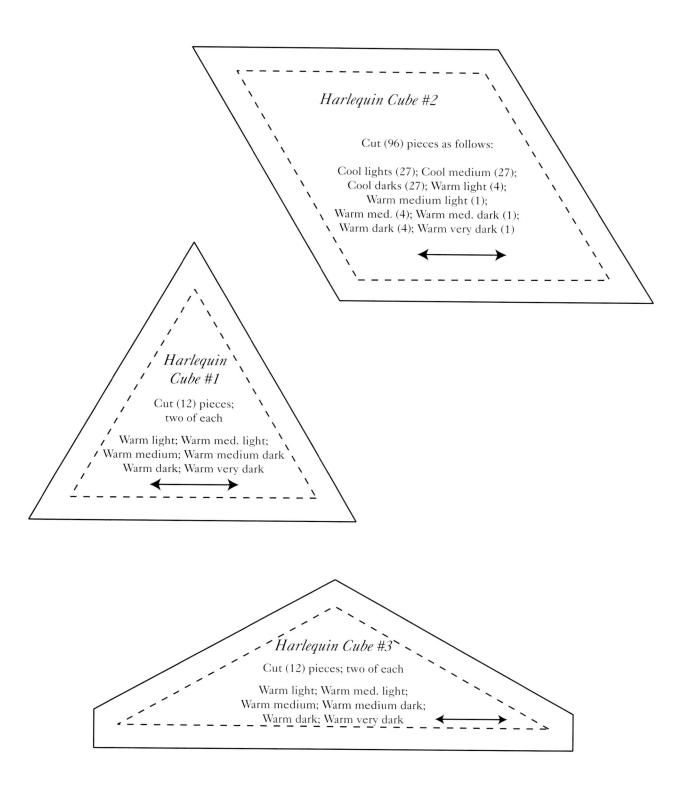

Harlequin Cube #2

Cut (96) pieces as follows:

Cool lights (27); Cool medium (27);
Cool darks (27); Warm light (4);
Warm medium light (1);
Warm med. (4); Warm med. dark (1);
Warm dark (4); Warm very dark (1)

Harlequin Cube #1

Cut (12) pieces;
two of each

Warm light; Warm med. light;
Warm medium; Warm medium dark
Warm dark; Warm very dark

Harlequin Cube #3

Cut (12) pieces; two of each

Warm light; Warm med. light;
Warm medium; Warm medium dark;
Warm dark; Warm very dark

Optical Illusions for Quilters

CONCLUSION

"Abstract ideas are the patterns two or more memories have in common. They are born whenever someone realizes that similarity… Creative thinking may mean simply the realization that there's no particular virtue in doing things the way they always have been done."

Rudolf Flesch

Toss a pebble into a pond and watch the circles form perfectly and spread effortlessly. You can think of your art as those circles. Circles of creative energy spreading out, taking in new ideas, reaching out for new experiences, but always coming back to the center — to you.

I hope you will take the ideas and information presented here and use them to create beautiful art, whether it be quilt art, fiber art, paintings, or drawings.

Each of you has been given a unique talent. Use it. Your art comes from you. I know you have heard it said that there is nothing new under the sun, but no one has viewed the world exactly as you have. Use that personal view to create art from your center, from your experiences. Each of us has the ability to take whatever it is that makes our lives unique and weave it together with our experiences and influences to create something that is original and fresh.

If you are willing to open yourself to all sorts of possibilities and are willing to risk traveling down untraveled paths, the possibilities are endless. It takes patience. Our lives are built one piece at a time, just as a quilt. It takes courage. We must believe in ourselves enough to seek what is truly our own voice.

Experiment, and don't be afraid to fail. The only people who do not fail are the ones who do not try. From your failures, art will come that is truly yours.

And may you truly become a "Master of Illusion."

"The bitter and the sweet come from the outside, the hard from within, from one's own efforts. For the most part, I do the thing which my own nature drives me to do."

Albert Einstein

GLOSSARY

After-image – An unusual visual sensation continuing after the stimulus causing it has ended.

Asymmetrical – Not symmetrical.

Chroma – Degree of intensity, strength, saturation, or purity of a color.

Closed form – That which echoes the form of the original and does not reach out into the surrounding space. The opposite of open form.

Field – A background on which something is drawn or projected.

Gradation – A sequence in which the adjoining parts are similar or harmonious. A regular and orderly change.

Horizon line – In linear perspective, the line where sky and earth seem to meet. It is on this line that the vanishing point is located.

Hue – A color.

Irradiation – The apparent enlargement of a bright object seen against a dark background, caused by a stimulation of the retina around the image.

Kinesthetic art – Art which seems to stimulate in the viewer physical sensations other than visual ones.

Multiple image – The use of the same visual element a number of times in the same composition.

Nonobjective art – Art that does not attempt to represent the recognizable form or effect of objects as they appear in nature.

Open form – Artwork, part of which projects into the surrounding space.

Op-Art – A style of art of the 1960s characterized by complex geometric patterns designed to create optical distortions, illusions, and the like.

Optical mixtures – Pure primary colors used in small touches side by side so that they seem to merge, producing secondary colors.

Perspective – A mechanical system of creating the illusion of a three-dimensional space on a two-dimensional surface.

Aerial or atmospheric perspective – Uses value and color modification to suggest or enhance the effect of space.

Linear perspective – Primarily linear in treatment. The science of representing objects in three-dimensional space with line on a two-dimensional surface.

Pictorial area – The area within which the design exists; generally of measurable dimensions and bordered by mat, frame, border or lines.

Picture frame – The outermost limits or boundary of the picture plane.

Picture plane – The actual flat surface on which the artist executes a pictorial image. In some cases the picture plane acts merely as a transparent plane of reference to establish the illusion of forms existing in a three-dimensional space.

Symmetry – Reverse repetition on opposite sides of a center or an axis, as in animals, insects, fish, and flowers.

Transparency – A situation in which a distant plane or shape can be seen through a nearer one.

Visual field – The total area visible to the unmoving eye at any given moment.

Volume – A three-dimensional shape that exists in space. On a flat surface the artist can only create the illusion of a volume.

BIBLIOGRAPHY

Beyers, Jinny, *Quilter's Album of Blocks and Borders*, EPM Publications, Inc. 1980.

Brackman, Barbara, *Encyclopedia of Pieced Quilt Patterns*, American Quilter's Society, 1993.

Birren, Faber, *Creative Color*, Van Nostrand Reinhold Company, 1961.

BlockBase™ version 1.0, The Electric Quilt Co., 1991 – 1995.

CorelDRAW™, Corel, Canada.

Diehl, Gaston, *Vasarely*, Crown Publishers, c1973.

The Electric Quilt Version 3.0 IBM, The Electric Quilt Co.

Ernst, Bruno, *The Eye Beguiled*, Benedikt Taschen Verlag GmbH, 1992.

Frisby, John P., *Seeing, Illusion, Brain, and Mind*, Oxford University Press, 1980.

Graves, Maitland, *The Art of Color and Design*, McGraw-Hill, 1951.

Gutcheon, Jeffrey, *Diamond Patchwork*, C & T Publishing, c1982.

Horemis, Spyros, *Optical and Geometrical Patterns and Designs*, Dover Publishing, c1970.

Howard, Constance, *Embroidery and Color*, Van Nostrand Reinhold Company, 1976.

Itten, Johannes, *The Art of Color*, Reinhold Publishing Co., 1961.

Lauer, David A., *Design Basics*, 3rd edition, Holt, Rinehart and Winston, Inc., 1990.

Locke, John, *Isometric Perspective Designs and How to Create Them*, Dover Publishing, c1981.

Luckiesh, M., *Visual Illusions*, Dover Publications, 1965.

Martinez, Benjamin and Jacqueline Block, *Visual Forces: An Introduction to Design*, 2nd edition, Prentice-Hall, Inc., 1988.

McKelvey, Susan, *Light and Shadows*, C&T Publishing, 1989.

Metzger, Philip W., *Perspective Without Pain*, North Light Books, c1992.

Mills, Elaine, ed., *Guiding Stars: A Sampler of Quilter's Favorite Quotations*, R & E Miles, 1989.

Montague, John, *Basic Perspective Drawing*, Van Nostrand Reinhold, c1993.

Norling, Ernest, *Perspective Drawing*, Walter Foster Publishing, 1989.

Ocvirk, Otto, *Art Fundamentals: Theory and Practice*, Wm. C. Brown Company, c1975.

Parola, Rene, *Optical Art, Theory and Practice*, Dover Publishing, c1969.

Powell, William F., *Perspective*, Walter Foster Publishing, 1989.

Smith, Ray, *An Introduction to Perspective*, Dorling Kindersley Limited, c1995.

Spies, Werner, *Vasarely*, Verlag Gerd Hatje, c1969.

Thurston, Jacquelin B. and Ronald G. Carrahen, *Optical Illusions and the Visual Arts*, Reinhold Publishing Corp., 1966.

Turner, Harry, *Triad Optical Illusions and How to Create Them*, Dover Publishing, c1978.

Watson, Ernest W., *Creative Perspective for Artists and Illustrators*, Dover Publishing, c1992.

Wolfrom, Joen, *The Magical Effects of Color*, C&T Publishing, 1992.

ABOUT THE AUTHOR

Karen Combs has worn many hats. Trained in library science, she has worked as a bookmobile librarian for Michigan State Library, in a small public library, and an elementary school library. She has also operated a home-based garment alteration business, a small quilt shop, and a mail order fabric business.

Karen became interested in quiltmaking in 1974 while still in high school and has been making quilts ever since. She is known for taking a traditional pattern and giving it her own unique twist. She has always been intrigued with quilts of illusions and has been designing quilts with the illusion of depth for the past five years.

Karen loves to share her quilt knowledge, teaching for quilt guilds and conferences nationwide, and was nominated for Teacher of the Year by *Professional Quilter Journal* in 1995. She is co-founder of Maury Quilter's Guild, has served several terms as president and vice-president, and published their newsletter.

Her quilts have appeared in many quilt shows and also been a part of the Silver Dollar City Wall Hanging Challenge, and the Hoffman Challenge.

Being a prolific designer and writer, Karen has published articles and patterns in many magazines, including *Quilter's Newsletter Magazine, Traditional Quilter, Quilting International, Traditional Quiltworks,* and *Lady's Circle Patchwork.* Working with Sharlene Jorgenson, Karen co-authored *3-D Fun with Pandora's Box* in 1997. She grew up in Michigan and in 1990 moved to the rolling hills of middle Tennessee where she lives with husband Rick, daughter Angela, son Josh, two cats, Gizmo and Benjamin, and at last count, four fish.

INDEX

INDEX

INDEX